Rifle

STEPS TO SUCCESS

Launi Meili

HUMAN KINETICS

Library of Congress Cataloging-in-Publication Data

Meili, Launi, 1963-
  Rifle : steps to success / Launi Meili.
      p. cm. -- (Steps to success sport series)
  ISBN-13: 978-0-7360-7472-8 (soft cover)
  ISBN-10: 0-7360-7472-4 (soft cover)
  1. Rifle practice. I. Title.

  GV1177.M45 2009
  799.3'1--dc22

                                    2008035866

ISBN-10: 0-7360-7472-4
ISBN-13: 978-0-7360-7472-8

The Web addresses cited in this text were current as of October, 2008, unless otherwise noted.

Acquisitions Editor: Justin Klug; **Developmental Editor:** Cynthia McEntire; **Assistant Editor:** Scott Hawkins; **Copyeditor:** Bob Replinger; **Proofreader:** Coree Clark; **Permission Manager:** Martha Gullo; **Graphic Designer:** Nancy Rasmus; **Graphic Artist:** Tara Welsch; **Cover Designer:** Keith Blomberg; **Photographer (cover):** AP Photo/Vincent Yu; **Photographer (interior):** Neil Bernstein; **Photo Production Manager:** Jason Allen; **Photo Office Assistant:** Joyce Brumfield; **Art Manager:** Kelly Hendren; **Illustrator:** Gary Hunt; **Printer:** Versa Press

We thank the United States Olympic Training Center in Colorado Springs, Colorado, for assistance in providing the location for the photo shoot for this book.

Human Kinetics books are available at special discounts for bulk purchase. Special editions or book excerpts can also be created to specification. For details, contact the Special Sales Manager at Human Kinetics.

Printed in the United States of America   10   9   8   7   6   5   4   3   2   1

Human Kinetics
Web site: www.HumanKinetics.com

United States: Human Kinetics
P.O. Box 5076
Champaign, IL 61825-5076
800-747-4457
e-mail: humank@hkusa.com

Canada: Human Kinetics
475 Devonshire Road Unit 100
Windsor, ON N8Y 2L5
800-465-7301 (in Canada only)
e-mail: info@hkcanada.com

Europe: Human Kinetics
107 Bradford Road
Stanningley
Leeds LS28 6AT, United Kingdom
+44 (0) 113 255 5665
e-mail: hk@hkeurope.com

Australia: Human Kinetics
57A Price Avenue
Lower Mitcham, South Australia 5062
08 8372 0999
e-mail: info@hkaustralia.com

New Zealand: Human Kinetics
Division of Sports Distributors NZ Ltd.
P.O. Box 300 226 Albany
North Shore City
Auckland
0064 9 448 1207
e-mail: info@humankinetics.co.nz

Rifle
STEPS TO SUCCESS

Figure 1.4   Determining Stock Length

CORRECT STOCK LENGTH

1. Move the butt plate in as far as it **will** go
2. Place the butt plate inside your upper arm as close to your elbow as possible
3. Reach your forearm up to the pistol grip
4. Wrap your fingers around the pistol grip

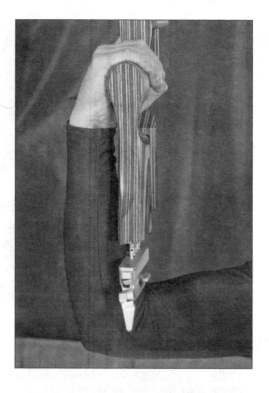

If you can easily wrap your fingers around the grip, the stock length of the rifle is at the proper starting point around which to build positions. If you can't reach the pistol grip, the stock length is too long (figure 1.5). Building positions around the extra length will be difficult. If you reach past the pistol grip and trigger, the stock length is too short. Add some space between the stock and butt plate.

Figure 1.5   Shooter is unable to reach the pistol grip, demonstrating that the stock length is too long.

JACKET AND PANTS

In three-position sporter shooting, a shooting jacket and pants are not allowed. This rule eases the way in the sport because you have to use your body to build positions and learn to hold the rifle with little support. When faced with challenges, you look to your body for correction and work hard physically to hold the rifle steady. In precision three-position air rifle shooting, you will need a shooting jacket and pants to compete at the higher levels. Revel in the fact that the hard work done when you weren't allowed to wear a shooting jacket and pants will pay off because your positions and ability to hold the rifle steady will improve quickly.

As with rifles, many brands of shooting jackets and pants are available. For shooters getting started, the best bet is to get a ready-made set in your size (figure 1.6). As you continue to advance in the sport, you may want to buy a custom-made jacket and pant set that specifically fits your body. These cost more but will last a long time if you take care of them properly. If you are still growing, you may want to wait to invest in custom-made jacket and pants until you either become very skilled and compete at a high level (where everyone else is getting additional support from their shooting gear) or haven't changed in body proportions for some time.

The jacket (figure 1.7) is made with padding running down the back of the arms and across one shoulder. The padding protects your body when you are in the prone position and using a sling and helps secure the butt plate into your shoulder. Jackets are made of leather or canvas and, when fitted properly, support your back when you are in the standing position. Jackets come in models for right- or left-handed shooters. This factor determines the placement of the

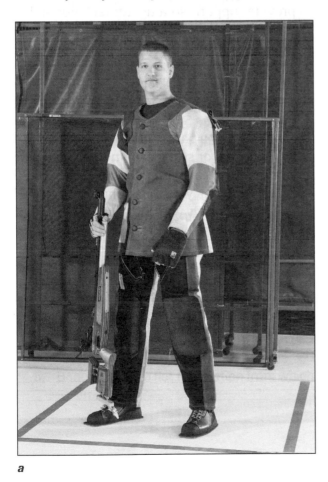
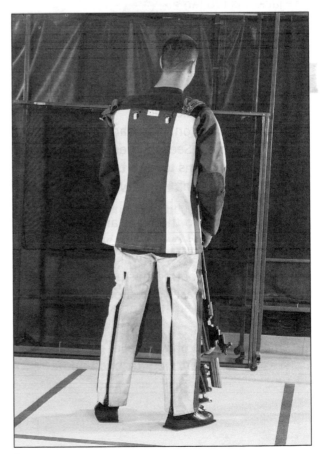

a　　　　　　　　　　　　　　　　*b*

Figure 1.6　Off-the-rack jacket and pants.

BOOTS

Shooting boots are not the most important piece of equipment when you first get started shooting, but after you reach a higher ability level and want to compete, they help significantly with stability and balance, especially in the standing position. Made specifically for this sport, shooting boots provide a flat surface from which to shoot without the sponge effect that you feel when shooting in tennis shoes. Shooting boots come up past the ankles to help reduce the amount of movement there, and you can open them up in the back to get into the kneeling position. Many people think that they look like cross-country ski boots, and they have a similar shape, but they are built for the specific purpose of ankle and foot support in rifle shooting.

Use a consistent kind of sock with your shooting boots. If you change to socks that are much thicker than what you normally wear, the boot will fit tighter and become more uncomfortable as you shoot. Shooting boots should fit the foot as any shoe does. They shouldn't press on any one part of the foot, but they should be snug enough that the foot doesn't move around in the boot. When trying on boots, lace the boot and assume a standing position. The outside pressure of the foot in the boot should be firm but comfortable. Get into kneeling position and be sure that the toe of the foot on the ground isn't pressing too hard against the front of the boot. Toes need some wiggle room for comfort.

Keep in mind that new boots take some time to break in. Your feet may ache at first while the boot forms to your foot. Just be sure that the boot is not too tight or small and provides a flat foundation to shoot from.

BELT

A belt can be worn with the pants (figure 1.8). Specific rules govern the width and thickness of the belt, so be sure to double-check that a belt is legal before you buy one and train with it. International rules require a belt to be only 40 mm wide and no more than 3 mm thick. Most other rule books follow this requirement. A belt supports your back and gives you a bit of a ledge to rest your elbow on when you are in the standing position. Some shooters choose to use suspenders because they like the feel of the suspenders crossing their backs. You are not allowed to use both suspenders and a belt, so try both to see whether either provides a better feel and support. Neither of these accessories is required, but either can be a help to support your standing position.

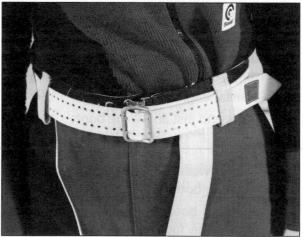

Figure 1.8   A shooter may choose to wear a belt.

GLOVES

You need a shooting glove to protect your hand, especially when you are in the prone or kneeling position. In these positions, you place your hand against the hand stop. A glove protects your hand from the pressure that is established in these positions, giving you good control of the rifle. Most shooters use a glove when in the standing position as well because the weight of the rifle presses straight down on either the palm or the knuckles. In some hand positions you may not need a glove while standing. We cover those in step 4.

Gloves are usually made of leather with padding on the inside and plastic or some kind of gripping and protective material on the outside.

Manufacturers offer different protective materials on the back of the glove. Some have fingers in them, and some have cut fingers. As with other shooting gear, you'll have to see what you like and then experiment. Try various gloves to learn what works best for you and your equipment. A right-handed shooter needs a glove only for the left hand; the opposite goes for a left-handed shooter. Rules govern how far the glove can come over the wrist and also prohibit having any closure device around the wrist, so be sure to look at the rule book before you buy a glove. Gloves that are available and used in high-power and other NRA events may not be legal in three-position air rifle.

HAND STOP AND SLING

These items go together to help support the prone and kneeling positions. The hand stop (figure 1.9) is placed on the rail under the fore-end stock in a location to establish the proper angle of the forearm in prone position and comfortable

Figure 1.9 Hand stop.

hand pressure. Hand stops of many different shapes are available, so try a few of them to see how they feel against your hand and whether they provide a secure fit. Some hand stops are shorter and compress the hand to the stock more tightly where the sling crosses over the hand and wrist. Some shooters like this tight fit. Shooters with larger hands may want a larger hand stop to fit into the web of the hand. A smaller or shorter hand stop may cause a shooter with a larger hand more pain. Try different sizes and shapes to find a hand stop that fits securely and causes less pain. The hand stop is usually placed in a different location for prone and for kneeling.

Slings are made of either leather or plastic. Plastic slings are harder to cinch up when you are in position, but they are a better choice because they don't stretch. Some are available with a tightening or loosening system built in so that you don't have to get out of position to adjust your sling.

The sling is placed on the upper part of the arm, secured by the jacket strap or hook, and attached to the hand stop (figure 1.10). Because the arm angles are usually different between prone and kneeling, the length of the sling will also be different. The purpose of these pieces of equipment is to stabilize the rifle by taking up the weight so that the sling arm can relax. If your sling arm and hand are tense and working to hold the rifle steady, then they are not in the right locations with the correct sling tension for support.

Figure 1.10 Correct placement of sling and hand stop in the kneeling position.

SCOPE

If you are shooting paper targets, you will need a scope to see your shots down range. If you are a right-handed shooter, you set up the scope just to the left of the positions and close enough so that you need to move only your head and not your whole body to look through it. If it's placed too far away, you will continue to move or roll toward the scope, weakening your positions every time you stretch to see through it. The scope magnifies the target and, when adjusted correctly, provides a clear picture of what's going on with shots. Be sure to set up the scope so that it is focused on your target, not your neighbor's target! Sighting in is tough when you're looking at someone else's shots. Most clubs have scopes, so you may not have to buy one of your own.

PRONE MAT

While in the prone position, shooters use a mat to provide a softer (and cleaner) surface for shooting. Mats usually have a padded area at the front where you can place your elbows so that they won't slip or easily move while you are in position. The mat is placed at an angle to the firing line because prone positions are shot from an angle. For a right-handed shooter, the top of the mat is angled to the right. Be sure to place your mat right up to the firing line. You want your elbow just behind that line, not on or across it. If you set your mat back a ways from the line, you not only compromise safety but also add distance to your target, and that's not in your favor.

Some clubs just use cut carpeting as mats. That's a good start, but if you want to train extensively and compete, get a mat that provides more padding for your elbows and a surface that won't slip around while you load and look through your scope.

KNEELING ROLL

Use a roll to help support your ankle and foot while you shoot from the kneeling position. The best kneeling rolls are cloth sacks filled with small plastic beads. A good roll acts like a beanbag under your instep and wraps up around your ankle for a little more support.

Many shooting clubs use rolled-up pieces of carpet. This practice isn't recommended because the ankle tends to roll on top of the carpet. Carpet isn't legal to use in some matches. Many premade kneeling rolls made of soft material or rubber conform to the rules. But if a premade roll isn't available, cut a 10-inch section off a straight pair of old jeans, sew a round patch to cover one end, fill it about three-quarters full of plastic packing beads, sew another round patch over the other end (be sure it's 7.2 inches, or 18.3 cm, in diameter or less), and you are good to go!

Kneeling rolls can be purchased or homemade. Check out the materials that they are made from. Some are nonslip, but few shooters actually fall off their kneeling rolls. The kneeling roll should be wide enough to come up around and support the ankle.

ADDITIONAL EQUIPMENT

Although most of the equipment discussed in this step is mandatory, here are a few more items that most serious shooters use.

- Offhand stand. For standing position, a shooter rests the rifle on an offhand stand between shots and while loading. The stand keeps the rifle high by the shoulder so that the shooter doesn't have to do a lot of lifting each time he or she positions the rifle to shoot. The stand also holds the pellets so that they are within easy reach for standing and kneeling positions.

- Timer. Many shooters place a timer on the offhand stand to help them keep track of how much time remains in the match. By using a timer they avoid being caught off guard and running out of time at the end.

- Hat or visor. When the lights at the range are overhead, many shooters use a hat or visor to shade their eyes so that they have a sharper sight picture in the bright light.

- Pellet holder. These special pellet containers protect pellets by holding each one in its own hole, preventing the pellets from being banged around during travel.

- Shooting glasses. For a shooter with corrected vision, the first choice is to wear contacts. But shooters who can't wear contacts need to get shooting glasses. Shooting glasses have a special kind of frame for just one lens to fit the needs of shooters who are shooting from different positions. Shooting while wearing regular glasses is difficult because the prescription is usually not in the right place for looking through the sights.

- Glove for the shooting hand. Some shooters like to wear a thin glove on the shooting hand to help grip the pistol grip. If your hands become sweaty while you are shooting, a glove may be a good piece of equipment to acquire.

TARGETS

In three-position air rifle shooting, you will be shooting at 10 meters on an official air rifle target (figure 1.11). If you are shooting in an NRA-sanctioned match, you will shoot on official NRA targets labeled either AR5/1 or AR5/10. If you are shooting in a match sanctioned by the National Three-Position Air Rifle Council (American Legion, BSA, CMP, Daisy/U.S. Jaycees, 4-H, USAMU, JROTC Commands, or USA Shooting), the official targets include NC-AR10 and any International Shooting Sports Federation (ISSF) air

rifle target. The host of the match is responsible for supplying the correct targets.

The most common targets are called 10-bull targets. They have 10 bulls, or black circles, going around the target. The two bulls in the center are called sighters. You use the sighters to sight in your rifle before going for record, or starting your match shots. Targets also have scoring rings. The center dot is called the 10 ring, although it's not an actual ring. It's called the 10 ring because the other rings are called 9 ring, 8 ring, 7 ring, and so on.

Some matches use 5-bull targets, and some have just a single bull. In matches that use single-bull targets, you'll change your target after each shot. Sometimes this is done manually and sometimes electronically.

Some ranges have electronic targets. Electronic targets are shot in international competition and in many college programs in the United States. If you are shooting an electronic target, you won't need a scope. The electronic version of the target is on a monitor by your point, and you won't have to worry about the scoring because the electronic system does it. In addition, you will be able to maintain just one position and will not have to move your natural point of aim constantly from bull to bull because you have just one aiming bull to shoot at. We will discuss natural point of aim in detail in step 6.

Figure 1.11 Official air rifle target.

RULE BOOKS

The NRA and the National Three-Position Air Rifle Council each have their own rule book for three-position air rifle matches. Fortunately, most of the rules are the same, but you should have a copy of the rule book for the matches that you plan to shoot in. Know the differences between the two and be prepared because rules can change on an annual or biannual basis. Training and competing with an outdated rule

book is a bad idea because many elements of the sport continue to evolve.

Most of the equipment that we have covered have rules related just to them. If you are buying, borrowing, or making some of your own gear (some parents out there have made shooting jackets and pants), be sure to check the rule books for accurate measurements for everything from length of jacket to thickness of belt and width of kneeling rolls.

SUCCESS SUMMARY OF SELECTING AND FITTING EQUIPMENT

After completing step 1 you should be able to identify precision air rifles and the accessories that go with them. You should be able to make good decisions about fitting the rifle properly through testing stock length and rifle balance. You should be able to assess the fit of shooting jackets, pants, and boots so that your clothing matches your body and is not too tight.

Before Taking the Next Step

Before moving on to step 2, Shooting Safely and Responsibly, evaluate what you have learned to this point. Answer each of the following questions honestly. If you answer yes to all six questions, you are ready to move on to the next step.

1. Have you acquired a rifle?
2. Have you begun to fit the rifle to your body?
3. Have you tested stock length and rifle balance?
4. Have you acquired proper clothing, pellets, mats, scopes, and other necessary equipment?
5. Have you become familiar with the different types of targets?
6. Have you read a rule book for the type of shooting that you want to do?

Shooting Safely and Responsibly

Shooting can be one of the safest sports if everyone follows the rules for secure gun handling and range safety. One of the most important characteristics you'll learn in shooting is respect, and you'll start learning about that in the beginning with safety. You'll learn to respect your rifle and equipment, the rules, and those around you. Safety is everyone's responsibility, and participants must always be aware of what is going on to ensure that the rules are being followed.

A moment of unawareness can cause serious injury, so everyone must follow the rules.

This step covers rifle safety and gun handling. We also cover range safety and your responsibilities when shooting on any kind of range.

Rules vary among ranges. Some ranges may have specific rules regarding lead safety, cleaning solvents and patches, or other issues particular for the area. Be sure to read and follow any posted range-specific rules when you are shooting in a new location.

HANDLING THE RIFLE

No matter what area or range you shoot on, safety rules are in effect whether you are alone or 100 people are present. The National Rifle Association has established fundamental rules that nearly every range and shooter follows. The NRA rules provide a good place to start when learning the basics, but be aware that other ranges and organizations may have additional rules particular to their location and match.

The following rifle-handling rules will keep you and everyone around you safe:

1. Always keep your rifle pointed in a safe direction (figure 2.1*a*). When on the firing line, point the rifle down range. If you are moving your rifle to the firing line, keep it pointed up.

2. Always keep your rifle unloaded until you are ready to shoot. Be sure that your action is open and that the breech is clear. You can also use a clear barrel indicator (CBI). Some organizations require shooters who participate in their matches or activities to use CBIs.

3. Always keep your finger off the trigger until you are in shooting position and ready to shoot (figure 2.1*b*).

Figure 2.1 — Handling the Rifle Safely

POINTING THE RIFLE

1. Always point the rifle in a safe direction
2. Point the rifle down range unless moving it to the firing line

FINGER OFF THE TRIGGER

1. Keep your finger off the trigger until ready to shoot
2. Place your finger on the trigger only when in shooting position

Rifles come with safeties. When you are finished shooting, check to be sure that the action is open (figure 2.2) and engage the safety. But don't take it for granted that having the safety engaged means that the rifle is safe and won't fire. Accidents happen when someone takes it for granted that her or his rifle is unloaded. Treat every rifle with respect and keep it pointed in a safe direction.

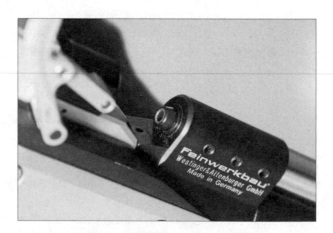

Figure 2.2 After shooting, make sure the action is open and the breech is empty.

CLEAR BARREL INDICATOR (CBI)

A safety practice required by the National Standard Three-Position Air Rifle Council and many ranges is that shooters must use a clear barrel indicator, or CBI. A CBI is a thick synthetic monofilament cord (like what's used in a line trimmer), and it's cut long enough that a portion can be seen coming out of both ends of the barrel (figure 2.3). Some ranges provide CBIs, but you should have one of your own and always keep it with your rifle. You can get the line at your local hardware store.

The CBI prevents anyone from loading the rifle. It provides visual proof that nothing, other than the CBI, is in the barrel. When you're finished shooting, and before you remove your rifle from the firing line, thread the CBI through so that the line officer can see it. You'll then be allowed to move your rifle from the firing line.

Figure 2.3 Rifle with CBI inserted.

RIFLE STORAGE

When you are in possession of a rifle, you assume the responsibility of storing it properly so that no unauthorized person has access to it. Store the rifle unloaded, with the safety on, and possibly a CBI inserted. Other safety devices are available and worth looking into depending on your situation and needs. A rifle can be locked in a rifle case and stored out of sight in your home, locked in a gun safe, or locked in an armory at your shooting facility. How you store your rifle depends on what is available and what level of security you wish to use. Just keep in mind that it is your responsibility to store your rifle safely.

RANGE SETUP AND BACKSTOPS

One of the important advantages to air gun shooting is that you can set up a safe range almost anywhere. Many serious shooters set up an air gun range in the basement so that they can practice to their heart's desire. All you need is a safe area where no one can enter from the sides or back and a backstop that will stop and contain pellets. Pellet traps (figure 2.4) are available from vendors, or you can create your own. One way to create a pellet trap is to place a sheet of steel angled at about 45 degrees inside a wood box with a tray to catch the shot pellets at the bottom.

Some shooters use a large box full of shredded paper and newspaper or chopped up rubber

Figure 2.4 Pellet trap that can hold two 10-bull targets.

tires to catch pellets. Be sure to have a secondary backstop to catch any shot that misses the main target area. This backstop can be a carpet hung up behind the target or a curtain of layers of canvas. Be sure that it isn't so tight that it causes ricochets. One of the best secondary backstops is dirt if you can shoot outside. Of course, you must practice all safe gun-handling precautions on a constant basis even when shooting at home.

Most ranges in communities, schools, military facilities, and international settings have an area for setting up, a firing point for each shooter, a firing line that is not to be crossed, and a target area with a pellet trap to stop and collect the spent rounds.

AWARENESS AND RESPECT

Be aware of the firing line. If anyone crosses the firing line while any shooting is going on, it is your responsibility to call, "Cease fire!" Anyone can call cease fire if someone crosses the firing line. More likely than not the range officer will correct anyone before he or she makes this kind of mistake, but safety on the range is everyone's responsibility.

If someone is already shooting and you plan to shoot on the point next to her or him, be courteous and wait for the shooter to complete the shot before you move your gear to the line. The same goes when bringing your targets back from down range. Wait for other shooters to complete their shots and then reel back the targets. If you are at a range where you must walk down range to retrieve your targets, wait for the cease fire command. The range officer will let everyone go down together to change or retrieve targets.

Another courtesy to observe on the range is to refrain from talking when others are shooting. Shooters will likely have earplugs in, so people tend to talk loudly to others on the range. You can certainly talk to the range officer or other person in authority if safety or competition issues must be identified and resolved. But don't use time on the range to catch up with someone or talk about your shooting. Take your conversation off the range so that you will not disturb people who are shooting.

SAFETY GLASSES AND EARPLUGS

Some ranges require shooters to wear safety glasses and earplugs. Although air rifles don't make much noise, you should get in the habit of wearing hearing protection. You will need earplugs if you shoot small bore or other higher calibers, and they are a great tool to help you block out voices and other distractions that may be going on around you while you're shooting.

Safety glasses are also a good idea. Safety glasses protect your eyes in case any pellets ricochet. Safety glasses are required on some ranges and in some matches, but not all. Whether they are required or not, wearing eye and ear protection is strongly suggested whenever you are on a shooting range.

SUCCESS SUMMARY OF SHOOTING SAFELY

Everyone on a range, whether shooting or not, bears the responsibility of maintaining safety. Following safety guidelines establishes respect for yourself, your rifle, the other shooters around you, and the sport in general. Accidents happen when someone takes it for granted that a rifle is unloaded. Treat every rifle as if it were loaded and act accordingly. This is your responsibility to everyone around you. Always keep your rifle pointed in a safe direction, unloaded, and your finger off the trigger until you are on the firing line and ready to shoot.

As you would like other shooters to respect you and your shooting on the line, be courteous to them as well. Keep your voice low if you must talk on the range, be considerate when going to the line when someone is already shooting, and bring your targets back after the shooters on either side have finished their shots. If you show respect first, others will follow. Respecting others fosters good sportsmanship and supports safety practices.

In the next step, you will learn about the parts of the rifle that shoot the pellet and how to adjust the rifle to fit into your positions better. You'll learn how to clean and maintain your rifle, and what to look for if something changes the way that the rifle fires. With a little care, your rifle will shoot well for years to come.

Before Taking the Next Step

Before moving on to step 3, Getting to Know the Rifle, evaluate what you have learned to this point. Answer each of the following questions honestly. If you answer yes to all four questions, you are ready to move on to the next step.

1. Can you recite the NRA's three safety rules for handling a rifle?
2. Have you acquired a CBI?
3. Have you become familiar with how to be courteous to other shooters on the line?
4. Have you acquired earplugs and safety glasses?

Getting to Know the Rifle

New technology and engineering have created rifles that perform to perfection. The air rifles that you see today are not your father's (or mother's) old Red Rider. These rifles are tuned so finely that they can shoot 10 pellets into a hole that has the appearance of being created by a single pellet. This step explains what makes these rifles unique to competitive shooting.

This step introduces many new terms that pertain to air rifles and how they work. You will learn about the parts of the rifle (figure 3.1) and how they function together to shoot a pellet. You'll see that many of the stock parts move and need to be adjusted to fit your body. After you can identify the parts of the rifle, the remaining steps in this book will be easier to understand and apply.

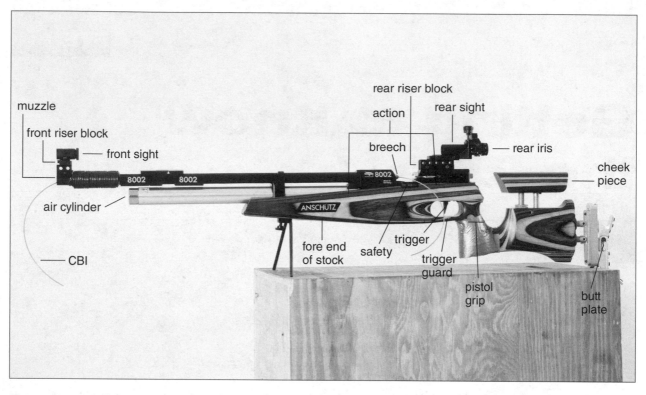

Figure 3.1 Air rifle.

ACTION

The action of an air rifle (figure 3.2) includes the air cylinder, the regulator, and the mechanism that opens the back part of the rifle where a pellet can be inserted into the barrel and fired down range (the loading area and breech).

The air cylinder (figure 3.3) is under the barrel and is screwed into the regulator. The air cylinder provides the power to shoot a pellet. The air cylinder is filled either by compressed air tanks (such as scuba tanks) or from an air compressor. A gauge at the end of the cylinder tells you

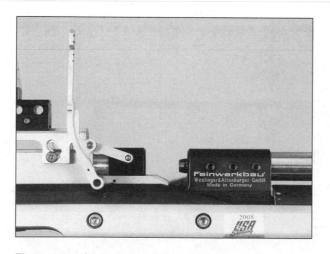

Figure 3.2 Action.

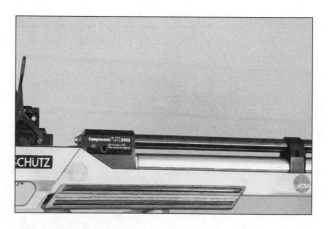

Figure 3.3 Air cylinder and regulator.

whether you have enough air or whether the air is getting too low to allow the rifle to shoot consistent shots.

To fill the air cylinder, unscrew it from the regulator, place an adaptor for your type of rifle onto a scuba tank or air compressor, and screw the cylinder into the adaptor. Slowly open the valve on the compressed air and let the pressures equalize between tank and cylinder. The air compressor turns off when the cylinder is full. After that occurs, close the valve on the tank, release pressure on your cylinder by opening the small valve on the adaptor, and unscrew your cylinder. Put the air cylinder back on your rifle, and you're ready to shoot again.

The regulator helps step down the pressure that comes from the compressed air in the cylinder. It reduces the air pressure to a standard amount so that the pressure is consistent for each shot. Consistent pressure ensures that shots are propelled at the same velocity and therefore shoot consistently on the target. Without a regulator, the shots being propelled from a full cylinder would be extremely fast, whereas those shot from an empty tank would be slow and dropping. Without a regulator on the rifle you could almost hit a different location with each shot because of velocity change.

The loading area (figure 3.4) is where the action opens at the back of the barrel, exposing the breech. The end of the barrel where the

Figure 3.4   Loading area and breech.

pellet is loaded is the breech. The action is then closed over the breech and pellet, and the rifle can shoot.

To load the rifle, pull back the cocking lever so that the action opens up to the loading area and breech. Pulling back the cocking lever also charges the rifle action with the correct amount of air pressure. Place a pellet in the breech and close the action over it. If you have an Anschutz or Feinwerkbau rifle, place the pellet right into the back of the barrel. If you have a Walther, place the pellet on the loading tray and use the bolt to load the pellet into the breech when the cocking lever is closed. When the trigger is pulled, the air charge is released and the pellet is propelled down the barrel and down range.

BARREL AND MUZZLE

The barrel is the long tube on top of the rifle. The end where the pellet leaves the barrel is called the muzzle. The inside of the barrel has rifling, twists cut into the barrel that cause the pellet to spin while in flight. This feature increases accuracy and improves consistency from shot to shot.

SAFETY

The safety lever (figure 3.5) is usually at the side of the action or near the trigger guard. The safety locks the trigger to keep it from firing. Use your thumb or finger to switch the safety lever from the fire position to the safe position while pointing the rifle down range. Engage the safety when you're not shooting but continue to treat the rifle as if it were loaded. Point it in a safe direction either down range or straight up when carrying the rifle to and from the firing line.

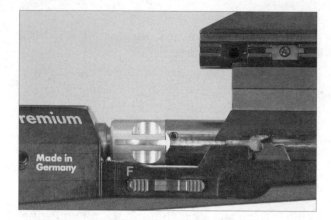

Figure 3.5   Safety lever beside loading area.

STOCK AND PISTOL GRIP

The barrel and action are screwed into the rifle stock. The rifle stock also includes the back of the rifle where the butt plate and cheek piece are located. Stocks come in many shapes and sizes and are usually made of wood, although some stocks are made of metal and plastic. Each has its own feel and balance. Try to hold as many different stock styles as you can to find what feels best for you.

The pistol grip is right behind the trigger guard and can be adjusted on many rifles. For adjustable pistol grips, turn the rifle upside down and locate a screw going into the center of the grip. Loosening that screw will cause the pistol grip to move toward or away from the trigger guard. Setting the pistol grip partly determines stock length. Moving the butt plate in or out has more of an effect on setting stock length, but adjusting the pistol grip can help fine-tune the fit. The farther back you move the pistol grip, the shorter the stock length is. This adjustment makes it easier for a shooter with shorter arms to reach the grip and maintain a comfortable position. One thing to be aware of is that this adjustment also moves the hand away from the trigger. Reposition the trigger so that your finger can reach it easily. We'll cover that topic in more depth later in the step.

TRIGGER AND TRIGGER GUARD

The trigger and trigger guard are directly under the action and in front of the pistol grip. The purpose of the trigger is to release the charged air in the action to propel the pellet down range. The trigger guard goes around the finger and trigger area to protect the trigger from accidental contact.

Some rifles have two rails that the trigger can be placed on. A shooter with smaller fingers should start by placing the trigger on the rail closest to the hand. A trigger can also be moved forward and backward on the rail so that the finger has a nice curved shape and the trigger can rest on the middle of the finger pad (figure 3.6a). If the trigger is too far away, the finger will be straighter (figure 3.6b). Shooting consistently is harder when your trigger finger is hitting the trigger from the side, and it could end up moving the rifle as well.

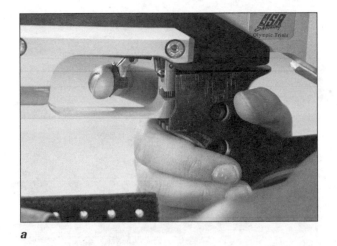

a   *b*

Figure 3.6 Trigger distance: (*a*) correct trigger distance—trigger finger is curved; (*b*) incorrect trigger distance—trigger finger is straight.

REAR AND FRONT SIGHTS

Rear and front sights are used to align the rifle properly with the target. The rear sight (figure 3.7) can be placed anywhere on the back rail of the rifle, but should be about 1 to 3 inches (2.5 to 7.5 cm) away from the eye when you are aiming at the target. Use the knobs on the top and side of the sight to adjust your groups on the target. Shooters refer to moving their sights by clicks. Different sights move different distances with each click. You will have to learn to adjust your sights by figuring out how many clicks it takes to move one ring on the target. Use this

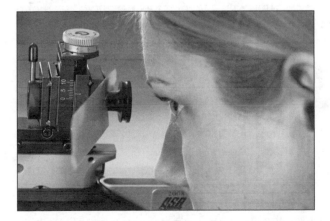

Figure 3.7 Rear sight.

information to get sighted in and to move your shots on the target.

Place the front sight even with the muzzle of the rifle. It is used to align the rifle with the target and must be in a fixed position. If the front sight gets moved or bumped, sight in again because the fixed variable in the aiming of the rifle has changed.

Your front sight may contain a cant indicator on the inside. These small lines made of wire show whether you are keeping the rifle level each time you assume your position.

Inside the front sight is an aperture that can be made of plastic, glass, or metal. The aperture has a ring in the center that is used to center on the target. Aperture rings come in different sizes. Be sure to have a variety of sizes because you will use a slightly smaller aperture size in the prone position as compared with standing. Different ranges have different lighting (indoors versus outdoors, too), and this factor can also affect the size of aperture that you use.

Riser blocks are used to get the sights up to the shooter's eye. No longer does the shooter have to bend the neck over to bring the eye and head down to the rifle when aiming. With riser blocks, the shooter's head can stay in a more upright position because the sights are brought up to the shooter's line of sight. The maximum height that you can use is 60 millimeters from the center of the bore to the center of the front sight. Some shooters use up to three sets of riser blocks. Riser blocks are a must for shooters with long necks.

Because ranges have different lighting, targets, walls, and backstops, an adjustable rear iris is helpful. The adjustable rear iris allows the shooter to control the amount of light getting to the aiming eye. It is used to help make the target look as sharp as possible and provide the most contrast between the ring of the front aperture and the target.

Some rear irises come with colored filters in them (figure 3.8). If you are shooting outside in bright light, filters help bring the color and contrast on the target under control. If it's dark outside, you can use other colors to brighten the contrast. Shooting indoors already eliminates a

Figure 3.8 Iris with filters. Each large notch on the side of the iris indicates a filter of a different color.

lot of light. Avoid using filters that continue to subtract light from the sight picture when shooting indoors. Some shooters find success by using a blue filter when shooting indoors.

CHEEK PIECE

The cheek piece (figure 3.9) is behind the action and sights and on top of the back part of the stock. The cheek piece is one of the best modifications to come along in air rifle shooting. Rifles today have a cheek piece that moves not only up or down but also right or left, or forward or back, depending on where the shooter needs it to be to

get into a natural position. So now the shooter's head can be more upright and better supported by the cheek piece than ever before.

If a shooter still thinks that the cheek piece could fit the contours of his or her face better, it can be sanded and molded to fit. You can do this yourself by starting with a regular piece of pine 2-by-4 (3.8 by 8.9 cm) cut into the shape of your basic cheek piece. Use a saw or sander to establish the angles and just keep sanding away until you have the shape that fits your cheek and face. Some shooters like a sharp angle to rest their cheekbones on; others like an additional groove cut in the front to rest on. Some take molding putty and try to make an exact fit to their face. After you complete the model, you can either finish the bottom of it so that it can be screwed onto your cheek piece base or sand and mold your current cheek piece after the model. This method gives you a sense of direction before you start cutting on your actual wood cheek piece. If all else fails, you can order a new one and start over if the shaping goes too far.

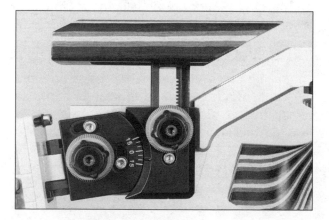

Figure 3.9 Cheek piece.

BUTT PLATE

The butt plate (figure 3.10) is at the far end of the stock and fits into the shooter's shoulder. Its purpose is to establish a secure fit of the stock into the body for control and stability. The butt plate is another useful modification for rifles. Compared with what shooters were using just 10 years ago, butt plates today fit the body better and are made to stay in place. They can be moved up and down, and right and left. A shooter can pull it out to create a longer stock or push it in to fit a smaller person's frame.

A word of caution: Butt plates can rotate on their axis. Be sure that the butt plate is straight up and down after you set it. You can shift it to the left or right on a straight plane with the stock, but you cannot tilt it to either direction.

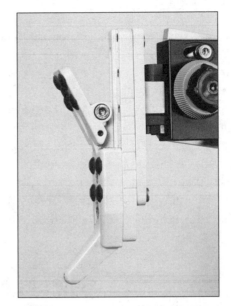

Figure 3.10 Butt plate.

RIFLE WEIGHTS FOR BALANCE ADJUSTMENTS

Many manufacturers make weights to fit their particular rifles. Be sure to get some rifle weights so that you can experiment with more weight at the end of the barrel, at the center of the barrel, or even at the back of the rifle. Rifle weights change the balance of the gun, allowing you to fine-tune the stability to fit the position that you want to establish. You can use weights made by the gun manufacturer to fit over your barrel or lead solder wire that you can wrap around your cheek piece base for added weight in back. You can also use the weights used to balance tires, which even have a sticky side that will aid in stacking them up under the cheek piece. Barrel weights slide on from the front, so you may have to take off the front weight and front sight mount. The other weights are designed to screw into certain screw holes already on the rifle. For that reason, a shooter usually has to buy weights that go with their particular gun.

BIPOD

The bipod (figure 3.11) is a small stand that a shooter attaches on the rail under the front end of the stock to support the rifle when it is not in use. The bipod keeps the rifle upright and protects the sights by keeping them away from the floor or from being bumped.

Figure 3.11 Bipod on a rifle.

RIFLE FUNCTION

The job of the air rifle is to shoot consistently, shot after shot. Usually human error causes a shot to go off its mark and end up someplace other than as a 10 on the target. The rifles most commonly used in three-position air rifle use a compressed air cylinder through which a small amount of air is stepped down from the air cylinder through the regulator and charged to a standard amount of pressure each time the rifle is cocked.

The regulator is a closed system. If you experience problems with consistency even when the air cylinder is full of air, have a trained gunsmith check it.

When the rifle is performing correctly, the charged air is stored in the action and used to propel the pellet to the target when the trigger is pulled. Because of rifling in the barrel, the pellet spins on its way to the target. The spin of the pellet produces consistent velocity and helps with accuracy so that the gun shoots in the same spot every time. Modern air rifles are more advanced than the rifles that had to be pumped 1 or 10 times to compress the air inside the rifle. Most air cylinders will fire about 200 shots before needing a refill, each with just a single cock from the loading lever.

RIFLE MAINTENANCE

Precision air rifles that are manufactured today are finely tuned technical pieces of equipment. Some shooters believe that their rifles are works of art, especially when they are shooting perfectly. Rifles will continue to perform to perfection when they are taken care of and properly maintained. Maintenance is an easy routine, requiring only some cleaning and protection from being bumped or banged around.

Cleaning the Rifle

Many theories exist about how often to clean an air rifle. In general, gunsmiths recommend cleaning air rifles after every 500 shots. If you feel that your rifle doesn't shoot as well after 300 shots, test it to determine whether the gun is performing properly. If it is not, clean it every 300 shots. You want your rifle to shoot to its full potential. If a bad shot appears on the target, you want to be sure that it came from your actions, not a problem with the rifle. Trusting your rifle and its ability to shoot at the same spot is important as you get serious about the sport.

Here is a list of supplies that you'll need to get started. You can find most of these items at any local sporting goods store that carries shooting supplies, but you may have to look harder to find the right cleaning agent.

- Cloth cleaning patches, 1 inch (2.5 cm) square
- Fishing line, about 20-pound (9 kg) test
- A cleaning agent such as TSI 301
- Cotton swabs such as Q-Tips
- A cleaning rag

To clean the rifle, follow the proper cleaning routine:

1. Cover the hole in front of the breech with tape (figure 3.12a). Be sure nothing goes into it.

2. If you don't have a factory cleaning line, double up a long section of fishing line. It should be long enough to go all the way through your barrel and have enough left over to wrap around your hand so that you can pull patches through your gun. Tie a knot at the looped end with enough of an opening in the loop to thread a patch through.

3. Open the action and thread the plastic line through from the breech to the muzzle (figure 3.12b).

4. Pull the loop to the breech and insert a patch that has been soaked in a cleaning agent (figure 3.12c). Avoid using the petro-

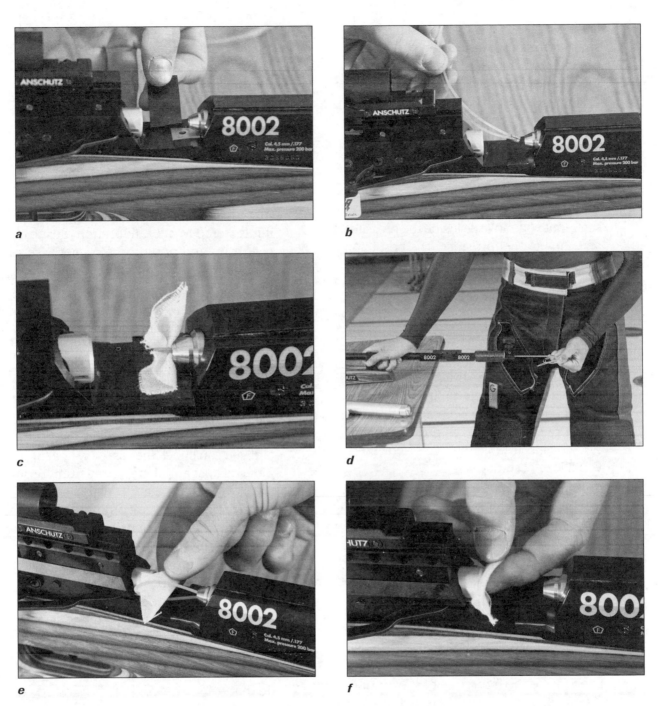

Figure 3.12 Cleaning the rifle: *(a)* cover the hole in front of the breech; *(b)* thread the line; *(c)* insert patch soaked in cleaning agent; *(d)* pull wet patch through muzzle; *(e)* after five wet patches, pull a dry patch through; *(f)* clean the chamber with a dry patch.

leum-based cleaning agents used to clean small-bore rifles, because they will corrode the exposed seals in the gun and require them to be changed. Non-petroleum-based cleaning agents are used to clean air rifles. The cleaning agent gets under the lead in the barrel so that it can be lifted out. If you have a small hole in the base of the action, be sure that no cleaning agent or oil gets into it. This hole leads to the regulator. Cleaning agents or oil can damage other seals that you can't see inside the regulator and can hurt performance. The best thing to do is to cover the hole with a piece of tape before you start cleaning. After you've finished cleaning, remove the tape and any remaining residue.

5. Pull the patch through with the line, bringing it out the muzzle end (figure 3.12d). Be sure to pull the line straight out the barrel. Pulling at an angle can rub the crown of the barrel and possibly damage it if a larger piece of debris is pulled out and scratches it. If the crown gets scratched, you'll lose accuracy.

6. Pull about five more separate patches through in this manner, each soaked with a cleaning agent.

7. Pull a dry patch through to see whether it comes out clean (figure 3.12e). If the patch is still dark with lead, repeat with a patch soaked in the cleaning agent and then try the dry pull-through again.

8. Clean around the whole action and breech with a clean patch (figure 3.12f).

9. Look inside the front tube of the air rifle. If you see dust or dirt there, either take the front tube off the rifle, if you can, and clean it out, or carefully use a patch or small cloth to clean around the inside of the tube. Just be sure that nothing goes back down the barrel and that nothing scratches the crown. This tube usually stays clean because of the air moving through it with each shot.

10. Check to see that all the exposed parts of the trigger are free of dust and debris. After the rifle has been used a while, even if it is stored in a clean location, dust can collect up and around the trigger. Use a cotton swab to clean the exposed area.

11. Every once in a while, take the barrel and action completely out of the stock and clean the areas that you can't get to with regular cleaning. Unscrew the bedding screws that hold the barrel and action in the stock. These are underneath the stock, so you'll have to turn your rifle over to find them. When the stock is removed, more of the trigger is exposed and you can check the rest of your action. Blowing dust and debris away from these areas with canned air available at office supply stores is not recommended. This method can blow debris right into the regulator and hurt performance. The best thing to do is use a rag or cotton swab to collect and remove what dirt you see. Then put the barrel and action back into the stock and replace the bedding screws. You need to tighten these screws down to a certain torque, and the instruction manual for your rifle will tell you how to do that.

Assessing the Rifle

When a rifle is not performing well, something may be wrong with the seals, which causes air to leak when the rifle is fired. You can usually change two seals yourself. The first is around the breech where the action fits over the opening for the pellet (figure 3.13). The second is on the air cylinder itself (figure 3.14). Both seals need to be working properly for the rifle to shoot. You will know when one of these seals becomes defective because your shots will go wide, you may hear a hissing of leaking air, or the rifle won't shoot at all.

Sometimes shots go low. Normally this occurs because of low pressure in the air cylinder, not a bad seal. Refill the air cylinder and you're back in the game. Don't wait until you see several shots go low before you check the level of air

Figure 3.13 Seal near breech.

Figure 3.14 Seal on the air cylinder.

pressure on your rifle. After one low shot, lower your rifle and read your air cylinder gauge. More likely than not, you'll have to get out of position and refill the air cylinder to the right level.

Packing for Travel

Traveling with an air rifle has fewer restrictions than traveling with a firearm. But airline personnel sometimes don't know the difference. Most likely your air rifle will be thoroughly checked because it looks like a small-bore rifle.

To get your rifle ready to travel, put the butt plate in a central location so that it isn't sticking out from the bottom of a soft case. This arrangement will help you get two rifles into a hard case and protect the rifle if it is knocked around. Take off the front and rear sights and put them in their own case where they will be better protected from being beaten up inside the rifle case.

Completely bleed out any air left in the air cylinder. Airline personnel could confiscate the air cylinder if any air is left in it. After bleeding out the air, put the cylinder back into the stock but do not completely tighten it.

For a small-bore rifle, many shooters just loosen the bedding screws when they travel. This precaution isn't as important with an air rifle because the stocks, torques, and bedding screws of an air rifle do not fluctuate as they do with a wooden small-bore stock. If you do decide to loosen the bedding screws, be sure to torque them to the proper tightness before you shoot again. Review the instruction manual for your rifle for proper torque on the bedding screws or have the rifle tested on a rifle-testing bench.

If you are traveling by air, you also want to pack your equipment bag strategically. Most shooters put the mat on the bottom, boots on one side, and offhand stand on the other side. Fragile items go in the middle, protected by the mat, boots, and stand. If you have a scope, be sure to put it inside a protective case. Anchor your scope rods so that they don't work their way out of even the smallest hole in your bag. Some people put them into their boot openings on each end.

Protect your sight box and pellet container in the center of your bag. You can use your shooting sweater or tights and glove to fill in any open spots. Neatly fold your jacket and pants and place them on top and you're good to go. If you have a hard-sided case, you don't have to worry as much about items being bumped and bruised. Even so, pack the case tight so that items aren't shaken up too much in transit. Airlines allow checked bags to weigh up to 50 pounds (22.7 kg). If bags are overweight, the airlines can charge an additional fee. Weigh your bags before you get to the airport and distribute the weight between your rifle case, equipment bag, and carry-on.

You may want to call ahead to the range where you'll be shooting to see whether they will let you borrow a prone mat and a shooting scope. If they will, your equipment bag will be lighter and your scope won't be beaten up in travel. Scope rods weigh a lot. If you aren't traveling with a mat, put your shooting pants or jacket in the bottom of your equipment bag as the first barrier.

If you are traveling by car, you can put your rifles in soft cases and secure them inside the trunk so that they don't move around. Be sure to take off your sights, however, to protect them from being bumped. You should still pack your equipment bag as if it's going into battle, with all the fragile items protected in the middle of the bag.

SUCCESS SUMMARY OF GETTING TO KNOW THE RIFLE

By going through this step, you have become familiar with all the working parts of your rifle and how they come together to shoot a pellet down range. Having an understanding of how the rifle functions helps you assess any change in the way that it shoots or identify a broken part. You should have no qualms about taking the barrel and action out of the stock and checking it to see whether it's dirty or whether a part has become loose. Many shooters are afraid to remove their stock, but that fear keeps them from knowing how their rifle works and how to fix it when needed.

You should now have a basic understanding of how the sights work and be open to all the variations that you can use to help them come up to your eye. Many beginning shooters lack this knowledge so they set up their positions incorrectly right from the start. Although all the equipment discussed in this step isn't mandatory for good shooting, you should at least conduct a trial to see whether it helps the rifle fit better or helps you see the target more clearly.

Taking care of your rifle is a priority if you want to keep it shooting well for years to come. After you get your cleaning supplies together, keep them in a spill-proof container in case the cleaning agent tips or a lid is not tightened down. Storing the items in a container also makes them easier to find when you want to clean your rifle.

Now that you have gained this knowledge, you can move into in-depth descriptions about what to do with the rifle when setting up positions and what to look for if something changes in the way that the rifle shoots. Ideally, this step gives you the confidence that you can properly care for and maintain your finely tuned piece of shooting equipment. If you take care of your rifle, it will take care of you in the way that it shoots and give you confidence on your shooting journey. In step 4 we will cover how to establish your shooting positions. The information in this section will help you build your positions systematically.

Before Taking the Next Step

Before moving on to step 4, Shooting Positions and Form, evaluate what you have learned to this point. Answer each of the following questions honestly. If you answer yes to all eight questions, you are ready to move on to the next step.

1. Do you know all the parts of the action?
2. Do you understand how each part of the action functions to shoot a pellet?
3. Do you know where the breech is?
4. Have you found out how many clicks per ring your sights move?
5. Have you discovered all the directions that your cheek piece and butt plate can move to help fit the rifle to your body and positions?
6. Have you acquired all your cleaning supplies?
7. Have you taken the barrel and action out of the stock?
8. Do you know what torque to use when tightening your bedding screws?

Shooting Positions and Form

To participate in three-position air rifle, you need to learn to shoot in the prone, standing, and kneeling positions. Each position has specific protocol and rules. Within the rules, you will learn to build a position with the rifle that fits your body size and shape. In the beginning, positions can feel unstable and challenging because you are learning an asymmetrical sport. Different parts of your body will be working harder than their counterparts do. But with work and refinement, your positions will become more comfortable and solid as you figure out the balance for each position.

When describing the shooting positions, we will cover two aspects: the outer position and the inner position. (For more on outer and inner positions, see *Ways of the Rifle* by Buhlmann and Reinkemeier, 2002, published by MEC in Dortmund, Germany.) The outer position takes into account the actual physical position of the body, including body angles to the target and angles associated with joints, hand positions, and leg positions. The inner position goes over where you should and should not feel tension inside your body, how to make the rifle feel tighter in a position, and how you should feel in general when the position is correct. The descriptions in this step are intended for right-handed shooters. Left-handed shooters just need to switch sides.

PRONE POSITION

Prone is the most solid position to shoot from because you have maximum contact with the ground and both elbows rest solidly on the mat. More ground contact means less movement in the position as a whole and more stability transmitted to the rifle while you're holding it. Prone is also a good position to learn to shoot from because your hold will be the steadiest and you will be able to control the movement of the rifle better than you can in other positions. This in turn will help with trigger control, follow-through, and shot calling. To become a consistent and good shooter from the prone position, work on these basic outer-position elements.

Lie on your abdomen on the mat (figure 4.1). (Note: Figure 4.1 and the following description is appropriate for a left-handed shooter. Reverse the directions for a right-handed shooter.) Position your body at a 10- to 20-degree right angle to the target. Keep your shoulders square so that they form a T with your spine, keeping in mind that this T will be angled 10 to 20 degrees from the target. Point your right foot straight or turn it in slightly. Draw your left knee slightly to the left. Extend your right elbow in front of your body and set it in front of your right shoulder. Angle the right forearm at least 30 degrees from the mat. Place your left elbow to the left and slightly ahead of your shoulder. Establish your right hand under the stock, resting against the hand stop. Wrap your left hand around the pistol grip. Your trigger finger can rest along the stock above the trigger guard. You are now in a basic position from which to adjust the rifle.

Figure 4.1   Prone Position

1. On abdomen, 10- to 20-degree right angle to target
2. Shoulders form a T with spine
3. Right foot pointed or in
4. Left knee slightly drawn up to left
5. Right elbow extended in front of body, in front of right shoulder
6. Right arm at least 30 degrees from mat
7. Left elbow to left of shoulder and slightly forward
8. Right hand under stock, resting against hand stop
9. Left hand on pistol grip
10. Trigger finger along stock above trigger guard

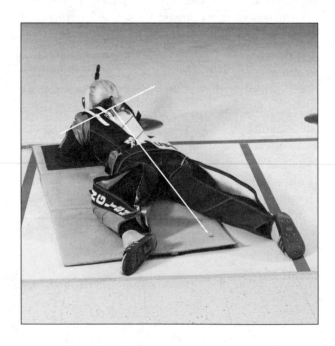

Before you hook up the rifle and bring it into prone position, make these adjustments so that you can more easily get it into your shoulder and make additional adjustments. It's tough to maintain the correct physical position if the gun is too long or the cheek piece is too high. If the rifle is set up for a previous shooter or just out of the box, the rifle could make your physical or outer position change, and that's not the correct procedure.

Before bringing the rifle into the prone position, make these adjustments:

1. Move the butt plate as high as it will go. If the butt plate starts low, it forces the cheek piece and sights to be far too high for shooting prone.

2. If the butt plate has one or two movable flanges that adjust the amount of curve around your shoulder, adjust the top one so that it's straight up and the bottom one so that it provides as much angle as possible to the butt plate. If the top one is adjusted for angle, it may keep the center part of the butt plate out away from your shoulder if it has the first point of contact. You want the center part of the butt plate to have the most contact with your shoulder and then move the top flange down to fit your shoulder after the center part is set.

3. Move the butt plate in as far as it will go. If the stock length is too long, getting the rifle into the proper place on the shoulder is difficult and the T shape of the shoulders and spine changes.

4. Remove the hand stop. You don't want to build your position around casual placement of the hand stop on the fore-end rail. If the hand stop is too far out, the rifle will point low and your arm may be less than 30 degrees from the ground. If the hand stop is too close, the shape of the T of the shoulders and spine could change. By placing the hand stop on the rail after establishing the correct position, you can see where the nonshooting hand needs to rest.

5. Place the rear sight forward on the rifle. Do this to get a natural head position on the cheek piece. If the sights are too far back, you'll have to pull back your head and neck to look through them. This head position isn't natural.

6. Start with the cheek piece in a lower position. If the cheek piece is too high, you'll angle or force your head down to look through the sights. You want to look straight out your eyes and keep your head level.

7. Use the right-sized aperture in the front sight. For prone position the right-sized aperture is somewhere between a 3.8-millimeter ring and a 4.4-millimeter ring, depending on your hold. If you start out with an aperture that is too small, keeping the bull inside it when you're holding on the target will be difficult. If you experience movement in the hold wide enough that the bull goes outside the aperture, the aperture needs to be bigger. The small aperture could teach you the bad habit of snap shooting or jerking the trigger because the sights are correctly aligned at the bull only for such a short time.

Adjust the rifle to your body. Trying to change your body to fit the rifle will only result in frustration. That frustration is common when a shooter tries to use a gun that was set up for another shooter. The rifle setup that works for one shooter rarely works for another. Think about what your outer position needs to be and then adjust the rifle to conform to that.

Rifle Placement in Prone Position

While lying on the ground, hold the fore end of the stock with your nonshooting hand. Using your shooting hand, place the butt plate on the inside of your shoulder. You can even place it on your collarbone to be sure that it's close to your neck (figure 4.2a). Set your elbow back on the mat and rest your shooting hand on the pistol grip. Now place your nonshooting hand in a position that raises the front of the rifle to the target. Rest your cheek on the cheek piece.

Close your eyes, take two or three breaths, and let the position settle. Open your eyes to see whether you are looking through your sights. If not, raise or lower the cheek piece until you are looking straight through the sights. Adjust your cheek piece by removing it from the stock and adjusting the screws, rings, or whatever your rifle uses to make height adjustments for the cheek piece.

After you have a basic head position that allows you to look through the sights without moving your head up or down, see whether you are pointed pretty much in the center of the target. If necessary, adjust your nonshooting hand so that you are. Have your coach or teammate mark that location with a pencil. Slide your hand stop back to that mark and tighten it just in front of the mark. You can tighten the hand stop with an Allen (hex) wrench or by hand, depending on the model and make of the hand stop.

Put the sling on your arm above your triceps on the back of your arm (figure 4.2b). Place the sling as high as it will go on your arm. Tighten the keeper, the loop around the sling that adjusts the opening, that is in front of your biceps so that you can get two or three fingers between the keeper and your biceps. Do not tighten it all the way up to your arm; leave a little room for comfort. Be sure that when you hold the other end of the sling with your hand, the opening is directly in front of your biceps. It should not twist above or under your arm, a circumstance that would cause your arm to twist in position and not lay naturally. Attach the sling to the hand stop and put on your glove. Slide your hand between the sling and the forend of the rifle. The sling should wrap under your hand so that your hand can rest directly behind the hand stop with the sling coming around from the side of your wrist.

Lay down on the mat and stretch your arm forward so that your elbow is in front of your shoulder (figure 4.2c). The arm must be in a vertical plane. The sling should be directly under your hand, helping to hold that hand against the stock. Using your other hand, place the butt plate into your shoulder and grasp the pistol grip. Let your elbow rest comfortably out to the side and slightly forward of your shoulder.

Place your cheek back on the cheek piece and evaluate the fit of the sling. The sling should be tight enough to take up the entire weight of the rifle. If your arm is working to hold up the rifle, tighten the sling. If you can't get the rifle into your shoulder or if it feels as if your nonshooting hand is being forced up into the hand stop, loosen the sling. You may need to move the hand stop forward a bit as well. Now that you have a glove on, you may need to adjust the location of the hand stop slightly to accommodate it.

After your arm feels comfortable and is not working to hold up the rifle, check the distance of the butt plate (figure 4.2d). You can increase the stock length by moving the butt plate out so that the butt plate is tighter to your shoulder. If you can easily rotate the rifle with your nonshooting hand when in position, the stock length is too short and you need to lengthen it. If the stock is forcing your shoulder back and your spine and shoulders no longer form a T, then shorten the stock by moving the butt plate in. This is also the time to check whether the butt plate is making full contact with your shoulder. If the center portion of the butt plate is making full contact with your shoulder, you can move the top flange down to rest against the top of your shoulder. If the center part of the butt plate is resting high on your shoulder and the top flange is up in the air, you can move the butt plate down some. But you don't want the bottom flange hanging down below the armpit. That bottom point of the butt plate should have contact in the base of the armpit to keep the rifle from shifting in the shoulder.

INITIAL PLACEMENT

1. Butt plate on inside of shoulder
2. Elbow on mat
3. Shooting hand on pistol grip
4. Nonshooting hand raises front of rifle to target
5. Cheek on cheek piece

a

SLING PLACEMENT

1. Sling on arm above triceps
2. Keeper tightened over biceps
3. Sling hooked into hand stop
4. Sling wrapped under nonshooting hand
5. Hand resting directly behind hand stop

b

PLACEMENT CHECK WITH SLING

1. Sling helping to hold nonshooting hand against stock
2. Butt plate in shoulder
3. Shooting hand grasping pistol grip
4. Elbow to side and slightly forward
5. Cheek on cheek plate
6. Arm supported by sling

c

(continued)

Figure 4.2 *(continued)*

CHECK OF BUTT PLATE

1. Butt plate tight to shoulder, inside the deltoid muscle
2. If stock length is short, move butt plate out
3. If stock length is long, move butt plate in
4. Center of butt plate in full contact with shoulder
5. Bottom flange at base of armpit
6. Top flange angle adjusted to fit top of shoulder

d

CHECK OF TRIGGER FINGER PLACEMENT

1. Trigger hits finger between middle of finger pad and first joint
2. Finger curls in front of trigger
3. Finger moves straight back when firing
4. Adjust trigger on rail, if necessary

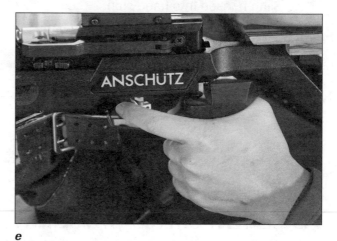

e

FINAL CHECK

1. Rifle to shoulder
2. Look down range
3. Check for neck or shoulder strain
4. Check for proper cheek pressure
5. Look directly through sights

f

The next item to check is placement of your finger on the trigger (figure 4.2e). You should be able to set your finger comfortably on the trigger so that the trigger hits your finger between the middle of your finger pad and the first joint. If the trigger is on the very tip of your finger, you will have to reach for the trigger and will most likely move your finger sideways instead of straight back. If your trigger finger does anything other than move straight back, you will lose an element of control and consistency when taking the shot. Some stocks have two trigger rails under the action. Select the rail that is closest to your hand so that it's easier to reach. You can easily move the trigger forward and back on the rail by loosening the one screw on its side.

Now that you have made the first adjustments of the rifle to fit your body, check the cheek piece and sight placement one more time. Put the rifle up to your shoulder and continue to look down range with your head off the stock. Close your eyes and place your head on the stock. Take a couple of breaths. Check for any strain in your neck or shoulders and cheek pressure. Open your eyes to see whether you are still looking directly through your sights (figure 4.2f). You may want to do this three or four times.

Beginning shooters find it a challenge to find a consistent head and cheek position because the feeling is new. After you find a general placement, adjust the cheek piece up or down, right or left, to get your eye directly behind the sight. After your eye is directly behind it, you can move the sight back so that it is 1 to 3 inches (2.5 to 7.5 cm) away from your eye. When adjusting the cheek piece, be sure that the sight is away from your eye. If the sight is too close, you will subconsciously keep your head back from the sight so you won't hit it. This placement is an example of the shooter trying to conform to the rifle instead of adjusting the rifle to conform to her or him. Keep the sight away from your face until you find a consistent and solid head position and then move the sight to it. When deciding how far the sight should be from your eye, you can also use the sight picture that you see in your sights. You want a consistent sight picture in each position, so a good rule of thumb is to have the front sight take

up about one-third of the sight picture. Some people move the sights so close to their faces that the front sight takes up only one-quarter of the sight picture. This is too small; it makes it hard to determine whether the front and rear sight are properly aligned.

Internal Characteristics of Prone Position

Prone will be your most solid position. You have the use of the ground, a sling, and both elbows. Focus on these factors to establish and repeat a solid inner position.

The left arm and hand should feel relaxed, as if they are just in place to prop up the rifle. The sling should do all the work of holding up the rifle. A high sling position on the arm makes this possible by providing more leverage. Your left arm should be so relaxed that your left hand and fingers don't have to grip the rifle. They should be free of tension and just resting against the stock. Many shooters don't even touch the rifle with the fingers of the left hand. They stay relaxed inside the glove.

You will feel tension in the front or web of your left hand where it meets the hand stop. You do need pressure here to establish a connection to the rifle and minimize hold. If the hand isn't tight enough against the hand stop, it will feel as if it's working to control the rifle. In addition, the left hand should not feel as if it is cocked to the right. The hand should be in a natural position with the rifle stock passing at an angle over the palm close to the thumb.

Place the elbows so that they feel as if they are forming a solid triangle under the rifle, not sliding out to the sides. If you feel your elbows wanting to slide out, bring them more under the rifle so that the pressure is directed down instead of out. Your elbows won't be directly under the rifle, but you'll feel that they are closer under the stock. The placement of your hand stop could be the issue if your elbows don't feel as though they are supporting the rifle. If the hand stop is too far back, the elbows can only go out when you are getting the rifle on target. If the hand stop is too far forward, the left arm will be straighter and not feel as if it's propping up the gun. If the position feels as if it wants to collapse, the hand stop could be part of the problem.

Your right hand should be able to grasp the pistol grip easily. If you feel as if you have to reach forward to get to the pistol grip, move your right elbow forward. If you still have to reach too far, look into shortening the stock at the butt plate. Ideally, you can just move the butt plate in to establish a shorter stock length. If you shorten the stock at the butt plate and now have very little shoulder contact, try moving the hand stop forward (away from the trigger) while leaving the sling length the same. This essentially slides the entire rifle backwards, increasing shoulder contact (pressure).

If you have an adjustable pistol grip, you can move it back as well. Be sure to follow that change by moving the trigger back so that you're not reaching for it with your trigger finger.

Another tip is to adjust your right knee. Moving the right knee up toward your elbow will tighten the feel of the rifle in your right shoulder. This adjustment will also lift your right hip off the ground, reducing the pressure on the abdomen area on the ground. Some shooters do this to help relieve the feel of the pulse in the hip and abdomen area. Some shooters like a straight right leg, so this technique won't work for them.

Check the feel of the trigger again. Resting your index finger on it should be easy. The trigger should touch between the middle of your finger pad to just inside the first joint. If you're reaching for the trigger, you'll most likely be out on the tip of your finger. The finger will look more straight than curved, and you will not be able to pull the trigger straight back.

Cheek placement is extremely important. Understanding the internal characteristics of the prone position will help you consistently put your cheek in the same place and be able to feel when it's not in the right place. Neck tension will tell you that your head is not in the right place, but it may take several shots before neck tension builds up enough to signal that things are incorrect (but your shots will tell you that right away). Double-check cheek placement by holding the rifle with your head off the stock and closing your eyes. Place your cheek on

the cheek piece with your eyes closed and just go through the upper part of your body to see that it's free of tension and that your neck feels relaxed. Identify the spot on your face where you want to feel the cheek piece. It's along the cheekbone at a place that falls naturally on the cheek piece. If you have to maneuver your face to look through the sights after you open your eyes, then the cheek piece is not in the right place and you need to adjust it again.

Also, have someone look at your position to see that your head is straight and that you are looking straight out of your eye sockets. That sounds strange, but some shooters tilt their heads down and look out of the tops of their eye sockets. This position becomes tiring. To correct it, lower the position at the elbows and move the hips back or raise the rifle in the position at the butt plate and hand stop.

When in prone position, you should feel relaxed throughout your body. You will feel pressure from the sling on your arm, on the hand stop, and on the butt plate at your shoulder. You will also feel some pressure in your cheek where it meets the rifle. All of these need to be equal and balanced and not so tight that they lead to tension in other parts of your body, such as your neck, shoulders, back, and arms. When you close your eyes while in position, the rifle should feel as if it could sit in that place for a long time. If it wants to fall in any direction, then you need to correct the foundation and reestablish the basic physical position.

Check to see whether you feel a large pulse during your hold. Beginning shooters often feel some pulse during the hold, but it shouldn't be so acute that it moves the rifle to the 6 ring. The pulse can come from a number of places where the blood flow through the arteries is being restricted. Check your right knee placement and raise it up a bit to alleviate pressure on your abdomen. Check the sling placement on your upper arm. You may want to raise or lower it a little to see whether that alleviates some pulse. You can also adjust the tension of the sling around your upper arm, making sure that the cuff is not too tight and that it's on the pad of the jacket. The sling tension going to the rifle may be too tight as well. Make sure that your glove is protecting your wrist and that your sling is wrapped about the back of your wrist and not cutting into it. Check the buttons on your jacket as well. Some prone shooters button only the top two buttons and move the rest of the jacket out of the way. Others button the jacket almost all the way down to keep it secure across their shoulders and back. Try both ways, but be sure that you're not lying on a button, which can cause discomfort and distraction.

STANDING POSITION

Standing position is shot without a sling, so developing balance and stability comes from many hours of holding, dry firing, and shooting rounds down range. But because the position has no sling adjustments or joint angles to work through, it's the easiest position to establish and repeat.

To begin to structure the outer standing position (figure 4.3), start by turning right 90 degrees to the firing line and centering your body in the center of your whole target. If you start by setting up your position to one side of the target, you'll have to exaggerate the upper-body twist to get centered or you won't have enough twist to support the rifle. Position your feet so that they are about shoulder-width apart. Keep your legs straight but not forced back at your knees. A critical detail is to keep your hips square to the target. This means keeping the alignment of your legs and hips in a vertical plane and oriented straight at the target. Your upper body then twists as a separate unit without rotating your hips, which would compromise the vertical plane, to point the rifle to the target. Any hip rotation requires leg muscle involvement to maintain stability, which will result in a left- and right-swinging motion as you hold. If you can keep your hips square, then you'll be able to use bone instead of muscle as support to stabilize the position.

Figure 4.3   Standing Position

1. Position centered in target
2. Feet shoulder-width apart
3. Body perpendicular to firing line
4. Legs straight
5. Shooting stand to the right at about shoulder height
6. Hips square to target
7. Butt plate near right shoulder
8. Left hand under rifle and close to trigger guard
9. Left elbow on or over left hip or slightly to the right on rib cage
10. Right hand gripping pistol grip with enough pressure to relax right arm
11. Head resting on cheek piece
12. Eyes looking straight

After your lower body is set, place the rifle either into the shoulder or out on the upper arm close to the shoulder and place your right hand on the pistol grip. Place your left hand under the stock, close to the trigger guard, in a position suitable for your height and strength. Using your left hand, arm, and back, lift the rifle and twist your upper body so that your upper body points toward the target. This action will bring the rifle up to your shoulder and the sight to your eye. Place your left elbow on the side of your body or slightly to the front if you can't make contact with your hip. Place your head on the cheek piece and look straight through your sights.

Make these adjustments to the rifle before setting up your position. This procedure gets the rifle ready for you to adjust it to your body, not your body to the rifle.

1. Check stock length to be sure that the stock isn't too long to start with.

2. Slide the butt plate down to the lowest position.

3. Move the butt plate in as far as it will go.

4. Move up the top flange on the butt plate so that it's straight.

5. Move the rear sights to a central position on the rail.

6. Use a 4.0- to 4.5-millimeter aperture in the front sight.

Rifle Placement in Standing Position

Assume the body position for the standing position (figure 4.4a). Place the rifle butt plate to your shoulder so that it is either set right into your armpit or just to the right on your upper arm (figure 4.4b). You may use either of these starting points. Try both to determine which is more comfortable, consistent, and stable for you.

After the butt plate is secure, grip the pistol grip with your right hand to maintain butt plate contact to your shoulder (figure 4.4c). Don't let the butt plate move around on your shoulder padding. Feeling changes between the butt plate and your shoulder padding is difficult, and any shifting can cause you to use a different head position on the cheek piece. If the rifle is close to your neck, you'll have a more upright head position. If the butt plate has moved out onto your arm, you'll have to reach for the cheek piece with your head and create more of an angle to the right. If the butt plate is lower on your shoulder, you will tilt your head forward and have to strain your eye muscles to look through the sights. Any of these changes will cause you to look through your sights from a slightly different angle because of the different head position. Different angles may look pretty much the same through your sights, but the change will affect your shots and they will not go where you call them or where you think they should be. A change in butt plate placement creates a chain reaction that can hurt performance.

Figure 4.4   **Checking Rifle Placement in Standing Position**

BODY POSITION

1. Feet shoulder-width apart
2. Hips square to target
3. Left hip pushing slightly toward target

a

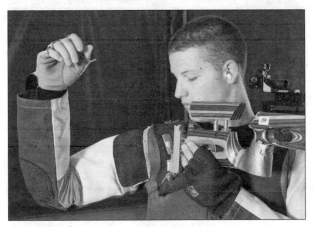

b

c

BUTT PLATE POSITION

1. Butt plate to shoulder
2. Butt plate fits comfortably and securely

RIFLE POSITION

1. Lift rifle
2. Elbow in position on hip or side
3. Hips in position
4. Rifle settles in direction of target
5. Face settles on cheek piece

After the butt plate is secure, place your left hand under the rifle, using one of the following hand positions. Try some of them to see what works best for your body and rifle.

• Fist position (figure 4.5a)—This position is best for shooters with short arms or long necks who need help to raise the rifle higher to the eye. While wearing your glove, make a fist with your left hand and place it under the fore-end stock close to the trigger guard. The contact point will be from the knuckles to the first joint. Try various angles at the wrist to see which angle gives the most support. Some shooters turn the fist to the side so that the fingers face to the right, others have the fingers facing straight back, and still others have them slightly to the left, which keeps the wrist perfectly straight. Just be sure to pick a position that doesn't cause the wrist to bend.

• Palm position (figure 4.5b)—This position is used when a higher rifle position is not needed. It usually feels more stable because fewer joints are involved in the position and it is easy to adapt to. With your palm up and fingers pointing to the left of the rifle, place your palm under the stock close to the trigger guard. You can try moving your palm more under the stock so that part of it is exposed on the right, or you can move it more to the left so that the wrist is directly under the rifle. It all depends on how the rifle balances on your palm and wrist, and it shouldn't feel as though it wants to fall off to the right. Some shooters use a glove with this hand position, and others don't.

• Grip position (figure 4.5c)—With the wrist straight under the rifle, the rifle rests between the thumb and fingers. Shooters with long forearms like to use this hand placement because it

a

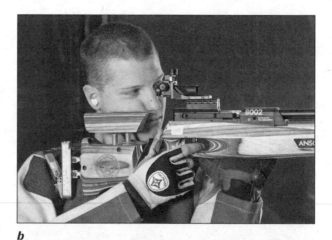

b

c

d

Figure 4.5 Hand positions: (a) fist; (b) palm; (c) grip; (d) split finger.

brings the rifle closer to the center of the whole position and not too high. Try it by placing your thumb to the left of the stock, your fingers to the right, and the web of your hand under the rifle. Be sure to bring your hand back toward the trigger guard because you'll end up using a lot of muscle to hold the rifle up if your hand is out too far.

- Split finger (figure 4.5d)—Less popular, but this position can help get the rifle higher to avoid having to bend the upper body forward. To use this position, turn your palm toward you with your fingers pointing up. Place the rifle between the first and third fingers and have the thumb pointing back toward the guard to provide a third point of contact. Alternatively you can lay the rifle between your fingers with your hand pointed down range.

After you decide on a hand position, place your hand under the rifle in the correct spot. The hand should not be so far out on the stock that the left-arm muscles have to work to keep the rifle up. The hand should be close to the trigger guard where you can get the most lift from the positioning, and the angle should be such that the weight of the rifle feels as if it is going straight from the wrist to your hip and then to the ground. Use as much bone support as possible in this position. Muscle involvement leads to a weakening hold, strain on your back, and low endurance.

To lift the rifle into place, start with the rifle resting on the shooting stand to the right of your position and the butt plate in place. Place your left hand under the rifle in the correct location and lift the rifle up and over so that you can place your elbow in the correct position on your hip or on your side.

Avoid getting your arm in position on your body before you lift the rifle. The lift accomplishes a couple of things simultaneously. It lets your hips move into the correct position without the arm and rifle getting in the way, and it lets your arm settle down in a consistent and secure spot each time. Trying to do all this with the rifle resting on the stand won't let you get into a consistent and natural position.

After your elbow is in the correct location, let the rifle settle in the direction of the target with your face off the stock. If you put your face on the stock before you lift the rifle or put it on when the rifle is aimed higher than the target, then the rifle, not your head and neck, is determining where your cheek will settle. To get a natural head position on the cheek piece, place your face on the stock after it has settled in the direction of your target.

With all positions, you want your head fairly straight and not tilting too far to the right. If you have to reach for the cheek piece with your head, you may need to offset the butt plate to the right to bring the stock into your body. You can also try canting the rifle into your cheek to help straighten your head (figure 4.6).

The next adjustment is to establish sight height. If you have a long neck and have to come way down to the sights to look through them, you may want to try riser blocks. Riser blocks

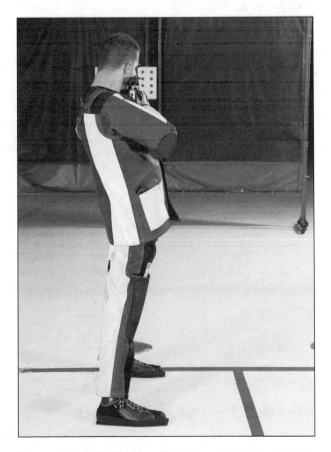

Figure 4.6 Adjusting the rifle to keep the head straight by canting the rifle.

are placed on the rifle, and then the sights are placed on top of them to help get the sights up to the eye so that the head doesn't have to go down so far. Almost everyone could use at least one set. Here's another way to paint this picture. With the rifle in position, the barrel is about level with your shoulder and the sights are only 1 to 2 inches (2.5 to 5 cm) higher than that. Because your eyes are pretty much in the middle of your face, you have to come down almost the full distance from eye level to shoulder level to look into the sights. That's a long distance, especially for anyone with a neck, which is everyone. So try riser blocks to help keep your head straight and level. Some shooters stack up three sets. Riser blocks come in various sizes, so try them to find what works for your position. Just be sure not to build the sights higher than 60 millimeters!

After you have established the sight height, adjust the cheek piece to allow a consistent and stress-free head and neck placement. To check the cheek piece, lift the rifle into place and look down range with your face off the cheek piece. Close your eyes and place your face on the cheek piece while keeping your eyes closed. Open your eyes to see whether you're looking through your sights. Move the cheek piece up or down and in or out until you are looking straight through the sights. If your head position doesn't feel comfortable, adjust the cheek piece until your neck feels free of stress but you still have firm cheek contact. Fine-tune the adjustments from there if you're close to looking naturally through your sights. If you are still far off from looking through your sights, you'll want to readjust the riser blocks to a height that's right for your more comfortable position.

Standing is definitely the easiest position to establish and adapt to. You don't have to deal with a pulse as you do in a sling position such as prone, and it is easy to adjust to point naturally at the target just by moving your feet.

Internal Characteristics of Standing Position

The standing position offers a lot of freedom. That characteristic can be beneficial because you will develop a strong sense of timing and intuition. Focus on these factors to establish and repeat a solid inner position when shooting standing.

Standing position is built on bone structure, not muscle. Many beginning shooters believe that they must use muscle to get the rifle into position and keep it there. After you learn what a good position feels like, you will find that the standing position is more a matter of maintaining balance and finding your natural point of aim.

With your feet shoulder-width apart and the rifle resting on the offhand stand, look down range at your target. See whether you're set up pretty much in the center of the target.

Before you lift the rifle, think about keeping your hips square to the target. Avoid rotating them toward the target. Beginning shooters tend to think about the challenge of holding the rifle steady, not aligning the body properly. Before you pick up the rifle, identify what your hips should feel like when they are square to the target. Push slightly toward the target with your left hip. Think of your left hip as a ledge for your elbow. Some shooters can reach this ledge; others cannot. If you can't, rest your arm on the side of your body.

Your back will be engaged in this position to help you maintain the proper upper-body twist, and it is displaced so that you can bring the rifle over the center of your body. When people talk about the standing position, many envision what a shotgun shooter looks like—forward lean, elbows out, gun in front of the body. The correct rifle position is nothing like the position of a shotgun shooter. In a rifle position, the body is upright, the upper body is turned, the rifle is brought into the center of the position, and the elbows are relaxed down. If you feel that a lot of muscles are engaged, as a shotgun shooter would, you need to check and adjust the foundation of your outer position. Only your back, right arm, and wrist should feel some engagement. If your neck, shoulders, left arm, legs, or feet have to contract to hold the gun still, keep working on your outer position and rifle adjustments.

KNEELING POSITION

In kneeling position (figure 4.7), you have to deal with a number of angles that come together to form a solid structure under the rifle. Because each body is different, no specific kneeling position is right for all shooters. Various arm, leg, and torso lengths create different options to use when setting up an individual kneeling position.

Figure 4.7   Kneeling Position

1. Centered to target
2. Left knee to left heel perpendicular to ground or slightly forward
3. Right ankle centered on kneeling roll
4. Right knee and toe flat on ground
5. Tailbone on top or in front of right heel
6. Hips and shoulders parallel
7. Left arm over or behind left knee
8. Sling high on left arm
9. Left hand behind hand stop
10. Right hand gripping pistol grip
11. Butt plate secure to shoulder

Before assuming the kneeling position, make these adjustments to your rifle so that you can more easily conform to your position.

1. Move the butt plate all the way in.
2. Move the butt plate to a central location on the stock.
3. Move the top flange up.
4. Move the sights forward on the rail.
5. Remove the hand stop.
6. Lower the cheek piece.
7. Use a 3.8- to 4.4-millimeter aperture in your front sight.

Rifle Placement in Kneeling Position

To establish the outer position, start by facing your target and centering yourself to it. Avoid setting up to right or left of center because doing so can cause the position to twist. Place the kneeling roll on the ground in the center area of the target at about a 45-degree angle to the firing line. Step forward with your left foot and kneel with your right ankle in the center of the roll and your right knee on the ground. Your right foot should be straight up and down, and your toes should be square to the floor, not tipping right or left. If your knee or toes are off the floor, adjust the location of the kneeling roll or reduce what is inside it to get closer to the ground. Your left heel and right ankle should be on a line to the center of the target.

Sit on your right heel so that your tailbone is in contact with your ankle (figure 4.8a). A straight line should run from your right toe to the top of your head (figure 4.8b). Sitting to one side or the other will cause the position to settle to that side, making you unbalanced from the start. In general, your positioning should be about 45 degrees to the target. Your left leg from your knee to heel should be straight up and down. For some shooters this position causes the left knee to be too high. If that is the case for you, angle your left leg slightly outward to the target to lower your knee. Now turn your foot so that your toes are slightly to the right.

KNEELING

1. Center to target
2. Kneeling roll on ground at 45-degree angle to target
3. Right knee secure on ground
4. Right ankle resting on kneeling roll
5. Right foot straight

a

b

STRAIGHT LINE

1. Tailbone in contact with right ankle
2. Straight line from right toe to top of head
3. Left leg straight from knee to heel or slightly out
4. Left arm and left thigh in line

c

RIFLE IN PLACE

1. Left arm over left knee
2. Sling high over left arm
3. Left hand behind hand stop
4. Butt plate to shoulder
5. Right hand grasping pistol grip
6. Face on cheek piece
7. Eyes straight ahead

At this point, your upper body should be angled about 45 degrees to the target and your left leg should be oriented straight toward it. Your left toe can be turned slightly to the right, and you should try to keep your right leg parallel with your left foot. Many beginning shooters think that opening up the kneeling position by angling the right knee farther to the right will provide more stability. In fact, this wider stance causes the rifle to move to the right after the shot. Try to keep your right knee in close to strengthen the position behind the rifle.

Place the sling high on your left arm and tighten the keeper in front of your biceps. Establish the correct arm angle again with your glove on and mark the rail under the stock. Place the hand stop just in front of the mark and hook up the sling. Place the web of your left hand against the hand stop so that your fingers are on the right of the stock and your thumb is on the left as in prone. The sling runs across the back of your hand and keeps it pressed against the stock. As in prone, your left arm should not be doing any work to hold up the rifle. The sling should be doing all that for you. If you are working to hold up the rifle, tighten the sling and perhaps move the hand stop toward you slightly to provide more of an angle.

Place your left arm over your left knee so that the flat spot on the back of your elbow rests on the flat spot of your knee. When you place your elbow out over your knee, your whole position will angle toward the target about 30 to 45 degrees. You can move your elbow around a bit to find the most comfortable and secure spot. Place your left hand behind the hand stop on the rifle and lift the butt plate into your shoulder with your right hand (figure 4.8c). The angle of your left arm should follow the angle of your left thigh, almost making a straight line from hand to hip. Your sling should be high on your left arm, taking up the weight of the rifle. Some shooters try a lower sling position. You may place the sling on or even below the triceps. Grasp the pistol grip with your right hand so that your right arm can remain relaxed and so that the butt plate stays securely in the shoulder.

Close your eyes and place your face on the cheek piece. Take a few breaths and open your eyes to see where you're looking. If you are coming way down to the cheek piece and sights, put on one set of riser blocks. You may want to add another set whether your head still has to come down too far. Close your eyes again and check to see with natural head and neck placement whether you can look straight through the sights. Move the cheek piece up, down, right, or left to get your natural head position directly behind the sights for proper alignment.

If you have long arms, try placing your left elbow in front of or behind your left knee. If you have shorter arms, try placing your elbow in front of your knee so that you can lean into the position more, providing more of an angle into the rifle for a lower center of gravity. Some shooters put the elbow behind the knee and have an upright torso and higher center of gravity. This arrangement can work for shooters who have longer limbs. Be sure to center your elbow over or behind the knee. Avoid placing it to one side or the other because doing so will introduce an additional angle to the position. Your left arm should point right to the target while resting on your knee. The ideal positioning of the rifle is almost directly over the elbow and knee, which is directly over the left foot. If you are looking into a mirror, you should be able to draw a straight line from the rifle down to the inside of the left leg to the foot without any extra angles to weaken the structure.

You should angle the left arm up to the point where it supports the rifle right to the middle of the target. An ideal angle would cause the left forearm and the left thigh to form a straight line. Again, this arrangement strengthens the position because bones support it, and it introduces fewer joint angles to break down. If the angle is correct between the left forearm and left thigh but you are aiming very high or low on the target, you can increase or decrease the filling in your kneeling roll to find the correct height. Avoid making extreme height changes with the hand stop and forearm under the stock. A straight left arm or one that requires a tight angle to get on target is an indicator that the foundation of the position is incorrect and needs to be adjusted.

A key factor when establishing the kneeling position is keeping the hips and shoulders parallel. If your shoulders are twisting to the right compared with your hips and your left shoulder is coming around closer to the rifle, you need to correct your position. This twist of the shoulders compared with the hips opens the position to problems of uncontrollable side-to-side movement and shots that will go right because of the twist of the shoulders and spine.

The head position in kneeling should be comfortable and level so that you are looking straight out your eye sockets. If you are leaning far forward and looking out your eyebrows, add a riser block and raise the cheek piece. Your butt plate will be positioned close to the center on the stock or slightly lower. If it is extremely high or low, check to see whether your kneeling roll is at an extreme height for your body size (either too large or too small). If it is, a chain reaction can occur throughout the position that ends with extreme settings on the rifle.

After you are in position, you should be able to draw a straight line from the top of your head to the toe of your right boot. If you can do this, your body is properly aligned and your bone structure is set to provide the best support. If your heel is going off to one side or your upper torso is leaning away from your hips, get out of position and set it up again without the rifle. Piece by piece, assume the full position again, keeping bone support intact.

Getting the rifle close to your neck can help in kneeling because the rifle is closer to the center of the whole position. If the rifle is too far out on your shoulder or offset to the right, the balance of the position shifts away from the center, and you'll fight your position the whole time. Either bring the butt plate closer to you so that it's resting on your clavicle or offset the butt plate to the right, which brings the stock closer to your head and neck. The butt plate can then be formed around your shoulder or whatever part of the jacket it fits best with in that area.

You should find it easy to grasp the pistol grip. If you have to reach for it, move the butt plate

in or move the pistol grip back slightly. Avoid moving the pistol grip and trigger between positions. Try to find a happy medium among all three positions for the pistol grip and the trigger and keep it there. You can move it, however, to find the best fit for this position because what works really well here may be close enough or not make that much difference for the others. Try everything and find the best standard for all three.

Internal Characteristics of Kneeling Position

Kneeling position takes a lot of structure building and rebuilding as well as training to develop a thorough understanding. This position has more body angles to deal with and more joints to support than the other positions do, but after you establish the position and train for a while, the kneeling position can be as steady as prone position. You need to spend a lot of time in the kneeling position to increase your stamina so that you can shoot for longer periods before you need to get up and out of position. You can also spend time with your eyes closed when warming up to get a feel for where your body is, where it wants to lean, and what stresses you feel inside the structure of the position. Focus on these factors to establish and repeat a solid inner position.

When you are in kneeling position, you should not have the feeling that your body wants to lean one way or another. If it does, start by checking your foundation. Your body should be about 45 degrees to the target, your left foot and right thigh should be parallel and about a foot (30 cm) apart, your left foot should be in the direction of the target, but the toes of your left foot should be slightly turned to the right. Your left leg from the knee to the heel should be either perpendicular to the ground or slightly forward. Your left leg should never be angled back toward your body because that configuration will introduce a weakness in the position.

To produce a comfortable kneeling position, the kneeling roll should be about half to three-quarters full. You can sit on your kneeling roll while watching TV to build endurance and comfort for longer shooting times.

In kneeling position, three points touch the ground: the toe part of the right boot, which should be flat on the ground, the right knee, and the left foot. Although getting your weight equally distributed among these points is challenging, no one point should be carrying most of the weight. If one point is carrying most of the weight, redistribute your balance by changing the kneeling roll, moving the kneeling roll, and shifting your position over your knee.

You can also check your left-elbow placement if you feel that your body wants to lean. You may need to move your elbow to another spot on your knee. Another item to check is the cant of your rifle. For some shooters, when the rifle is straight up and down it can lean to their right, away from the body while holding. Many shooters like to have the rifle cant into the head and neck to help balance the head angle of the position and bring the rifle closer to the eye. Because you can't adjust the angle of the butt plate on an air rifle, you have to cant the rifle yourself and be sure that it stays in the same location and at the same angle on your shoulder pad.

Some shooters have a tough time getting into a kneeling position, if the elbow is way out over the knee. This situation is usually caused by a sling that is too short or a hand stop that is too far out. If this isn't the case, shooters may try to shoot with the elbow behind the knee. This technique can work if the shooter has a solid position with the butt plate and can adequately manage the hold. If your position is too straight up and down, however, you won't have enough strength behind the butt plate and the movement during the follow through will be inconsistent.

If you choose to shoot with your elbow in front of your knee, when you reach out to place your left elbow your body will lean forward into the position. To avoid feeling a pulse from your hips or abdomen, fasten only the top two or three buttons on your jacket. You also want the front of your pants to be open and not constricting your abdomen in any way. The back of your pants should be unzipped and pulled out at the side by your knees to get as much fabric as possible away from the back of your leg. With all this maneuvering of jacket and pants you may wonder what help they give the position in the end. Be assured that although we get the fabric out of the way of the position, the pads on the knees, rear, and elbows provide substantial comfort when shooting. The jacket and pants also provide support in the hip and shoulder area, which is a big help to the position.

Place the butt plate of your rifle inside your shoulder. Most shooters like to have the butt plate on the inside of the deltoid muscle so that it stays securely in the shoulder and is close to the neck and face. With this position, you can add a cant and you don't have to lean your head toward the cheek piece. You can therefore keep your face upright.

As with the other positions, close your eyes while looking down range. Place your face on the cheek piece so that your neck and head feel comfortable. When you think that your cheek pressure is correct, open your eyes to see whether you are looking directly through your sights. Double-check that your head is not tipped down and that you are looking directly out the center of your eye sockets. If this is the case, then the height of the cheek piece is probably OK. If you are tilting your head down, raise your cheek piece until your head is level and you are looking straight out your eye sockets. If adjusting your cheek piece this way causes you to look above your sights, add riser blocks to your rifle to bring the sights up to the level of your eye. Most cheek pieces also adjust right and left. After a couple of trials to see where your head naturally rests, move the cheek piece right or left to center your eye directly behind your sights.

Some cheek pieces do not adjust right or left. If you have this kind of cheek piece and need to add width, try using tennis grip tape or moleskin. To subtract width, some shooters sand the cheek piece to make it fit the face better. Remember to practice molding a model cheek piece before you cut your permanent one. Many advanced shooters have a unique cheek piece for each rifle and even for each position that they shoot. You probably won't need this kind of dramatic change in the cheek piece, but you should know that these options can help in the future.

Many shooters become caught up in trying to create as long a stock as possible. They think that a long stock fits tighter in the shoulder, but making the stock too long causes difficulty in reaching the pistol grip, creates tension in the right arm, and causes the upper body to twist to the right. As you start training in the kneel-ing position, if tension forms in your right arm or shoulder, let go of the pistol grip and let your arm rest naturally. See whether you can bend your arm up without stretching forward to reach the grip. If you have to reach forward to get to the pistol grip, then you have found the source of your tension. On the other hand, if by rotating the left hand, the butt plate moves easily in your shoulder, go ahead and add some distance to lengthen the stock.

SITTING POSITION

Sitting position is shot in some NRA matches, usually with a small-bore or high-power rifle. If you have the chance to shoot in one of these types of matches, here are some position tips to help you get ready.

Sit on a mat facing the target with your ankles crossed in front of you (figure 4.9). Position your body at a slight right angle to the target, about 30 degrees. Place your elbows inside your knees. Your elbows will act as a brace to support your upper body. The hand stop will likely be closer to you than it is in prone position. Use the hand stop to help you lift the rifle to the center of the target. The sling will be shorter than it is in prone position to help support the rifle. The sling should be on the upper part of the arm, above the triceps. Place the rifle directly into the shoulder. Rest your face on the cheek piece. Your head will probably have a bit of a downward tilt to get the eye to the sight.

Start with these basic rifle adjustments:

1. Move the butt plate in as far as it will go and center it.
2. Move the hand stop farther back than it was in prone position.
3. Set the sights farther forward on the rail than they were in prone position.

Figure 4.9   **Sitting Position**

1. Sit on mat facing target
2. Ankles crossed in front
3. Body at slight right angle to target
4. Elbows inside knees
5. Sling above triceps on left arm
6. Butt-plate over armpit
7. Head resting on cheek piece

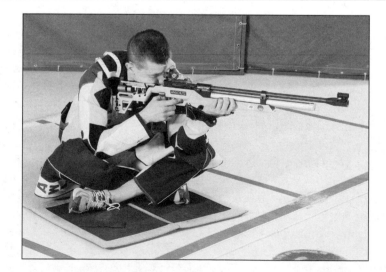

Rifle Placement in Sitting Position

You'll want to have only the top two or three buttons fastened on your jacket. Open the front and back of your pants as well so that no material cuts into your abdomen or legs. After you are in the basic position, put on your glove and hook up the sling. Wrap your hand under the sling and place the web of your hand on the hand stop as you do in the other positions. Using your right thumb, place the butt plate on the inside of your shoulder so that the bottom of the butt plate goes into your armpit (figure 4.10a).

Figure 4.10   Checking Rifle Placement in Sitting Position

ASSUME SEATED POSITION

1. Fasten only two or three buttons on the jacket
2. Open front and back zippers of shooting pants
3. Glove is on and sling is hooked up
4. Hand wraps under sling and grips the stack
5. Butt plate on inside of shoulder

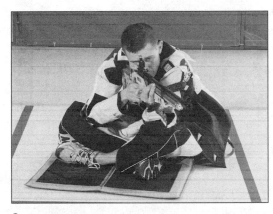

a

MOVE RIFLE INTO PLACE

1. Settle elbows on knees
2. Grasp pistol grip
3. Rifle points at center of target

b

LOOK THROUGH SIGHTS

1. Lower face to stock
2. Head is comfortable
3. Cheek rests on cheek piece

c

Settle your elbows on your knees and grasp the pistol grip with your right hand (figure 4.10b). Look to see that this basic position is slightly angled to the center of the target. If not, take the rifle down and adjust your sitting angle. Center the seated position naturally before getting too far in the position setup. Because the rifle has to come down and you need to use your hands to adjust your seat, establish that first.

After your natural point of aim is at the target, double-check the tightness of the butt plate in your shoulder. If your left hand can easily move the butt plate out of your shoulder, lengthen the stock. If you can't reach the pistol grip without strain, shorten the stock.

Lower your face to the stock (figure 4.10c). You'll find it difficult when sitting to get an upright head position. You'll most likely have to lean forward and down to reach the cheek piece. If this is uncomfortable, add a riser block or two. After your head feels comfortable, close your eyes and see whether your natural head position allows you to look straight through the sights. If not, adjust your cheek piece so that you can sight correctly.

Now check to see where you are pointing on the target. If you're too high, move the hand stop out or lower the butt plate, which causes the muzzle to go lower. If you are too low on the target, bring the hand stop in, tighten the sling, or move the butt plate up, causing the muzzle to rise.

Internal Characteristics of Sitting Position

Shooting while sitting can be fun because it's an easy position to get into and not part of normal training activities. Sitting position can be a bit more free moving than prone position because you are introducing the lower part of your body into the equation when establishing the position. Instead of the ground, you use your knees to support the rifle. Because most people can't get their knees to touch the ground in the cross-legged position, you will have a little more spring to the feel of this position. Focus on these factors to establish and repeat a solid inner position.

Secure your elbows inside your knees to provide the best support. Feel free to move your feet forward to change some of the height of your position, if necessary. Make sure that the sling is doing most of the work to keep the rifle up. In sitting position, however, your right arm will also do some work to help keep your position stable. The right arm can do this because it is anchored on the inside of the right knee. Relax your head and neck. You may have to go forward more in this position with your head on the cheek piece. This is normal and only causes you to move your sights forward. Keep them about 1 to 3 inches (2.5 to 7.5 cm) away from your eye. You may feel tension in your lower body. Do what you can to relax but remember that your knees are doing some of the work to stabilize your upper body so you should expect some tension. If the tension becomes too great, take a break, stretch your legs, and see whether you can establish a better position with your ankles.

Although sitting position is not shot in international matches, you may have the chance to shoot it in some NRA matches and have some fun with it.

SUCCESS SUMMARY OF SHOOTING POSITIONS AND FORM

Shooting positions are the foundation for your entire shooting journey. They will be the focus of most of your training and the factor that either makes or breaks your performance. After moving through this step, you should be able to establish each basic position and have a clear understanding of what makes up the outer and inner positions so that you can explore each of those aspects in training.

Each position has unique characteristics that make it challenging and fun. Prone is the most solid position, and you can expect great scores to come from shooting it. Standing is the freest position and helps you gain control over your body and learn to use your intuition when taking a shot. Kneeling uses different angles of the body to build a strong base and teaches balance and stability. Sitting provides variety and fun.

This step on shooting positions is important because you have to focus on what is going on behind the firing line first. When sights and a target are added to the equation, many shooters cease to focus on what is happening with their bodies and positions and think only about what is going on beyond the firing line, at the target. Now that we have covered the outer and inner positions, we can move on to the next challenge—how to aim the rifle correctly, what to look for in your sight picture, and how to adjust your sights to move your shots on the target.

Before Taking the Next Step

Before moving on to step 5, Aiming and Adjusting the Sights, evaluate what you have learned to this point. Answer each of the following questions honestly. If you answer yes to all six questions, you are ready to move on to the next step.

1. Have you established the outer-position characteristics for each position?

2. Have you adjusted your rifle to fit your body after assuming a natural outer position?

3. Do you know why you should close your eyes before placing your face on the cheek piece to check head placement and cheek piece height?

4. Do you know why you should keep your shoulders and hips parallel in kneeling position?

5. Are you able to repeat the same position when you get in and out of it a few times?

6. Have you tried the sitting position to use in various types of matches?

Aiming and Adjusting the Sights

This step shifts your attention to what you want to see when taking a successful shot. Because of the many details involved, we will address one element at a time. Then, when you're ready to take an actual shot, you will have a plan of action in place and will be able to assess what is happening and what you need to improve. These basic elements will later teach you how to time your shot and build a complete shot plan when shooting in competition.

EYE DOMINANCE

Before a beginning shooter ever picks up a rifle, the first thing that most coaches check is eye dominance. Everyone has a dominant eye, the one that does most of the work and sometimes focuses better than the other does. In the past the general belief has been that you should shoot from the dominant-eye side. So if your right eye is dominant, then you should shoot from the right side. But this may not be the best approach for shooters who are cross-dominant, those who write with one hand but have the dominant eye on the other side. In the past most coaches would just teach a cross-dominant shooter how to shoot from the dominant-eye side. But today, because shooters wear blinders over their nonshooting eyes, it really doesn't matter which eye the shooter uses. The logical approach is to shoot from the side that you are more coordinated on. Most right-handed people struggle when trying to learn to shoot from the left side because their eye–hand coordination is not as developed. Training the right eye is easier than training the eye–hand coordination on the other side of the body.

Do check your eye dominance, but don't use it as an absolute. Start out on the side that you write with. If for some reason you really struggle to see through your sights or experience a lack of coordination, then change to the other eye and learn to shoot from that side. Many people are cross-dominant; if you are, don't become locked into thinking that you can shoot only from your dominant-eye side.

Remember, although many coaches use eye dominance as an absolute indication of which side to shoot from, I encourage you to use the side that you are most coordinated from and train your eye to shoot.

Checking Eye Dominance

While keeping both eyes open, point to an object on a far wall with an index finger. Now close one eye. If you are still pointing at the object, the open eye is your dominant eye (figure 5.1). Open both eyes. Now close the other eye. If your finger moves off the object, then the open eye is your nondominant eye.

Figure 5.1 Testing eye dominance.

SHOOTING BLINDER

A shooting blinder (figure 5.2) is a small piece of plastic, paper, or anything that conforms to the size rule that you use to cover your nonaiming eye while you are shooting. Some shooters attach them to their sights; others attach them to their visors or shooting glasses. A shooting blinder allows you to keep both eyes open while shooting and relieves any stress in the facial muscles that could be caused by trying to hold one eye shut while aiming.

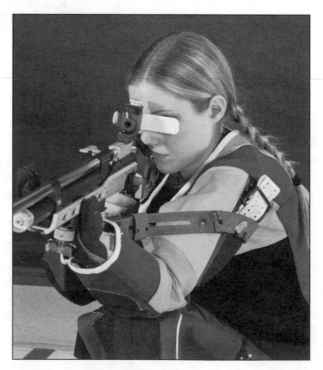

Figure 5.2 Shooting blinder.

EYE RELIEF

Eye relief is the distance from your eye to your front sight. Setting eye relief is critical after you have established your shooting position. Many shooters start with their sights already on their guns and in turn move their heads behind their sights and think that their head positions are correct. This circumstance is another example of fitting the body to the gun, not the gun to the body.

You must build or adjust your gun to your body and establish correct eye relief specifically for each shooting position. After you establish good head placement and the cheek piece is aligning your eye directly behind your sight, you can move the sight forward or back to get it within 1 to 3 inches (2.5 to 7.5 cm) from your eye (figure 5.3). Avoid getting the sight too close to your eye. As positions settle, most shooters tend to move the head slightly forward on the cheek piece. The natural position may well be more forward on the cheek piece. If this is the case for you, then the sight is keeping your head

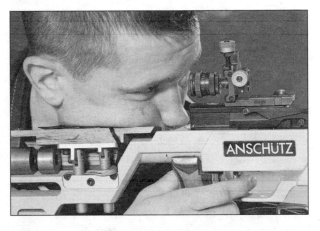

Figure 5.3 Good eye relief, sight 1 to 3 inches (2.5 to 7.5 cm) from eye.

back from where it really needs to be, not only causing neck tension but also causing you to place your face differently on the cheek piece as you try to find a more comfortable position. In turn, you have to look through your sights from different angles, resulting in different hits on the target.

SIGHT ALIGNMENT

Now that your sights are in the proper location, you need to learn to align them. Proper alignment includes centering the front sight inside the entire opening of the rear sight (figure 5.4). A rule of thumb, presented in *The Ways of the Rifle* (Buhlmann and Reinkemeier, 2002), is that your front sight should take up about one-third of the total field of vision inside your rear sight. You can move your rear sight forward or back to establish this point as long as it's within the 1-3 inch range from the eye.

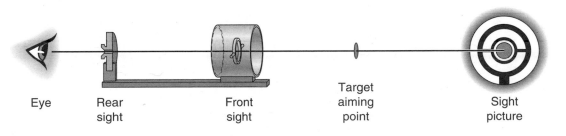

Eye   Rear sight   Front sight   Target aiming point   Sight picture

Figure 5.4 Front sight centered in opening of rear sight.
Courtesy of the National Rifle Association of America.

SIGHT PICTURE

Now that the sights are properly aligned, you can add the target. Having a correct sight picture means that the target is centered inside the front aperture (figure 5.5). Proper sight alignment and sight picture include three rings of light. The outer ring of light is the ring between your rear and front sight. The second ring of light is inside your front sight, and the third ring of light is the white around your target inside the aperture. When all these rings of light are centered, you know that your gun is pointed in the direction that you want to shoot.

After shooters add the target to the sight picture, they often neglect the alignment of the rear and front sights. You can have a perfectly centered target inside the front aperture and squeeze off a shot that feels like a perfect 10. But when you look through the scope you see a 9 or 8. The shot is off call because the rear and front sights were not aligned. Many shooters overlook this alignment. They become caught up in wanting to be sure that the target is centered and forget to check where the front sight is inside the rear sight. Having a systematic checklist or shot plan will help you account for all the elements that go into a perfect shot.

A word on aperture sizes. Many shooters are confused about what size the front aperture should be. They go for the smallest aperture they can find because they believe that shooting is easier when the aperture is close to the size of the target. This is a misconception.

When learning to shoot, you must be able to see the whole target hold inside the aperture ring. Therefore, use a larger aperture to get started. For beginning shooters, apertures for air rifles should range from a 4.0-millimeter ring to a 4.4-millimeter ring, depending on your hold. If you have a good hold in the prone position, then a smaller aperture is fine. But using that same small aperture with a larger hold, such as in standing position, can reinforce poor trigger control. Many shooters learn to snap at or jerk the trigger as the target passes through the aperture because it's inside the ring for such a short time. A large aperture allows you to see the whole hold and its movements inside it, and you can develop better timing and trigger control as you watch and anticipate the sights and target lining up correctly.

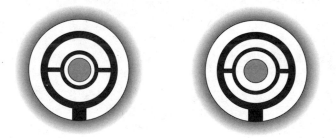

Figure 5.5 Target centered inside front aperture.

Sight Picture Drill.   *Supported Position*

Now that you understand the elements of aiming a rifle, let's get behind the rifle and put it all together. For this drill, use your rifle from its basic settings without a hand stop or sling. Move the butt plate to a central location. Be sure to use some kind of blinder on your nonaiming eye so that it can stay open. Many beginning shooters have to work hard to keep the nonaiming eye open, and this is a great place to start.

For the drill, place a table and chair on the firing line or set up a table anywhere it is safe to aim your rifle. Put a target down range or on a wall you can aim at. You won't be shooting at this point; instead you will be learning the basics of aiming and looking correctly through the sights. Place a kneeling roll on the table and sit behind it. Place the fore end part of your stock stock of your rifle in the center of the kneeling roll so that the rifle is supported and not moving around. Place your left hand under the front of the stock either in front of or behind the kneeling roll and place your left elbow on the table. Put the butt plate into your shoulder. Place your right elbow to the right of the stock and your right hand on the pistol grip.

Lower your body so that you can rest your face on the cheek piece (figure 5.6). You may have to slide the chair back. Maintain a straight back and lean forward at the hips. This position will permit you to look straight out of your eyes, not up through your eyebrows. Don't sit up straight and then curve your back to get your head down to the sights.

With your head resting on the cheek piece, look through the sights. Identify how much of the opening in the rear sight is taken up by the front sight. This area should be about one-third of what you see. Identify when the front and rear sight are aligned correctly, when the front sight is right in the middle of the rear sight. Now adjust the whole rifle onto the target. You may have to move your chair side to side to get the right angle.

Try to line up all three circles—the opening in the rear sight, the front sight, and the ring around the target. Practice taking your face off the cheek piece and then putting it back on and lining up the sights 10 times or more.

If your air rifle can be dry-fired and you are on a safe range, go ahead and squeeze the trigger after the sights are properly aligned to dry-fire some shots. Dry firing means going through the motion of shooting but without loading a pellet in the rifle. You'll do a lot of dry firing in training. In the next step, we'll go into more detail on trigger control, but you can start to combine more elements as you master sight alignment.

Figure 5.6   Supported-position drill.

SIGHT ADJUSTMENT

When sighting in the rifle, you are trying to move your groups to the center of the target. You want to avoid aiming your gun in any direction other than at the center of the target. To get your shots into the center of the target, you must move the sights.

Shoot a three- to five-shot group. See where this group lies on the target and then click your sights to move the center of the group to the center of the target. Do this by clicking the knobs on your sights (figure 5.7). To move the group up, use the knob on the top of your sights and click in a counterclockwise direction. To move the group down, turn the same knob in a clockwise direction. To move the group to the right, use the knob on the side of your sights and click it counterclockwise. To move the group to the left, use the same knob but click it clockwise. Some manufacturers use opposite direction sight adjustment knobs. Make certain that you know which way your gun's sights move.

Many manufacturers make sights. Many rifles already have sights with them. Because manufacturers vary and quality varies, sights will have a different number of clicks per ring. A high-quality sight may have 10 clicks per ring. A lower-quality sight may have only 3 or 4. (By

Figure 5.7 Clicking the sights.

ring, I mean the distance between the 8 and 9 rings on the target or between the edge of the 10 ring (or dot) ring and the center of the 10, for example.) You need to learn how many clicks per ring your sights move. When you're in a match and need to adjust your sights, you want to be able to click your sights right into the center of the 10 ring.

Sight Adjustment Drill.   *Sighting In*

Use the same setup for this drill that you used for the supported-position drill. Be sure that you are on a safe range and allowed to shoot. Support the rifle with a kneeling roll or sandbag and wear a blinder on your nonaiming eye.

Set up your rifle on the kneeling roll and adjust your body and rifle so that everything points at the target. Practice aligning your sights and just relax. See whether you stay pointed at the target when you relax. If you move, adjust your chair and elbows so that you naturally point at the target.

Load your rifle and take five shots at one bull. Note whether you made a group. If you didn't, shoot another five-shot group at a different target. If you've formed a group, identify the center of that group. Click your sights up or down, right or left to move the center of the group to the center of the target.

At first, you may have to guess how many clicks to use. If your sights are high quality, start with 6 to 8 clicks per ring; for lower-quality sights, use 3 or 4 clicks per ring. Take an educated guess and click your sights. Be sure to keep track of how many clicks you use in each direction.

Take another five shots at a different bull. Note whether you formed a group and whether it is closer to or over the center. This test gives you a better idea of how far each click moves the group on the target. Add more clicks or take a few off to center the group better. Keep track of the number of clicks that you use so that you have a good idea of how to adjust your sights. Shoot one more group and note whether it's over the center of the target. Remember to keep the rifle on the kneeling roll for the drill. Move your body around to keep it naturally pointed at the target in the supported position.

SUCCESS SUMMARY OF AIMING AND ADJUSTING THE SIGHT

In this step you learned how to set up your sights, what to look for in your field of view, and what proper alignment means. You need to practice to be sure that you have established each of these factors before going on to the next step and aiming. As our attention moves from the shooting position to the sights, our focus shifts from behind the line to the target, usually never to return. But you must be sure that the foundation is solid before moving on. With aiming, be sure that the front sight is centered in the rear sight before moving on to centering the target inside the front aperture. This approach also helps verify that your head is in the same position. If you consistently have trouble getting the front and rear sights to align properly when placing your face on the cheek piece, you need to go back and work on building a solid and consistent position because something is shifting your head and neck.

After head placement and rear and front sights are aligned, you are finally ready to think about getting into that 10 ring and shooting good shots. The amount of movement that you have in your hold is critical to determining the correct aperture size. Be sure that you can keep your entire hold pattern inside the aperture so that you learn to squeeze, not jerk, the trigger.

In the next step, you finally get to shoot some lead down range. You'll learn more about naturally adjusting your positions to the target before you shoot, controlling your breathing to help manage your hold, and developing trigger control to manage timing of the shot. These are the basics needed to shoot successfully. Master one element at a time, and then we'll put them together for a smooth shot process.

Before Taking the Next Step

Before moving on to step 6, Taking the Shot, evaluate what you have learned to this point. Answer each of the following questions honestly. If you can answer all eight questions, you are ready to move on to the next step.

1. Do you know which of your eyes is dominant?
2. Does this factor determine what side you shoot from?
3. How far should the rear sight be from your eye?
4. Why do shooters use blinders?
5. How much of the rear sight picture should the front sight take up?
6. Why do you want to use an aperture that contains your whole hold pattern?
7. How would you move your sights up, down, right, or left?
8. How many clicks per ring do your sights move?

Taking the Shot

Because you have reached this point, you should have a strong foundation on which to build, one stacked with all the elements of successful shooting. In this step, you will learn in depth about rifle parts—how they work together and what you should expect when making changes for a better fit to your body. Before you take a shot, we will go back to how positions feel and how you can adjust them so that you naturally point at the target that you want to hit. Putting a lot of energy into shooting a good shot is pointless if the foundation is wrong to begin with.

You will slowly build a checklist of all the foundation elements that you need to confirm before you take your shot. If one of those elements is off, then the likelihood of shooting a good score goes down with it. Take some time to write a list of all the important elements that you've learned so far so that they don't go by the wayside when we add more irons to the fire.

In this step, we'll cover natural point of aim and how to adjust it in each position. Again, this is the foundation that you need to establish before you even start thinking about what is going on down range. After you accomplish that, we'll cover what goes into creating a good hold, how to have good trigger control, and how to time your shots. When shots start going through the bull, you'll want to be able to call them so that you know whether it's you or the sights that aren't adjusted properly. Learning how to follow through will help tie it all together, and you'll be ready for some serious training.

NATURAL POINT OF AIM

Establishing natural point of aim is a technique that all shooters must do so that they are naturally pointing their positions to the center of the target. Natural point of aim (NPA) is where the rifle naturally points when held with a biomechanically sound position that uses maximal bone support and minimal muscle power. Set up your position and pick up your rifle just as if you are about ready to fire a shot. Instead of loading, however, let the rifle settle in position and put your face on the stock. Close your eyes and take three breaths. Open your eyes to see whether you are pointed naturally at the target. Also note whether your position feels balanced and stable and not as if it wants to drift in any direction. If you are not naturally pointed at the target, you need to move your whole position around its pivot point, not just the rifle in your position.

Adjusting Natural Point of Aim in Prone Position

In prone position, the pivot point is the left elbow for right handed shooters. When you shift your position (figure 6.1), your left elbow remains in the same place and your body rotates around it. If you are pointing left on the target, move your hips to the left, followed by your legs and right elbow. This movement will naturally adjust your position to the right. Avoid leaning the gun to the right. Because the gun doesn't want to point naturally in that direction, it will come back to the left as you fire the shot and your shots will also come back.

If you are pointing to the right of the target, reverse this tactic and shift your hips to the right followed by your legs and elbows. If you are pointing too high on the target, shift your hips forward. If you are pointed too low, shift your hips back.

After you've made your adjustments, close your eyes again and take three breaths. Open your eyes to see whether you are now naturally pointed at the target. You may still have to make some fine adjustments, but you should be willing to take time and energy to get everything in your position adjusted to the center of the target.

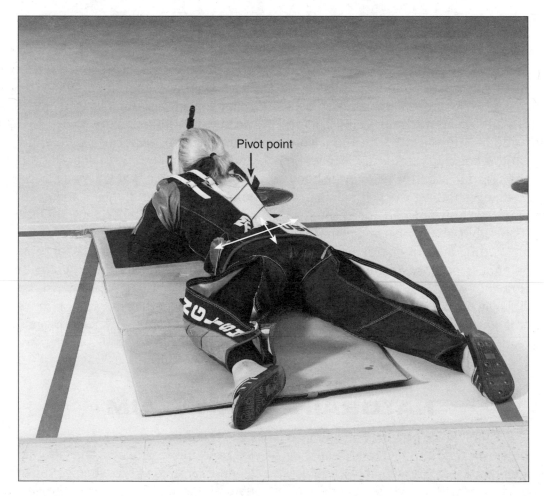

Pivot point

Figure 6.1 Natural point-of-aim adjustments in prone position for a left handed shooter with a right elbow pivot point.

Adjusting Natural Point of Aim in Standing Position

If your position is centered to the target in general, your left foot will be the pivot point of your position. To check your natural point of aim, pick up the rifle let it settle, and assume your position with your face on the cheek piece. Close your eyes and take three breaths, trying to relax in your position as much as possible. Open your eyes to see where you're pointing.

If you are naturally pointed to the right of the target, move your right foot slightly forward, and your left foot slightly backward (figure 6.2). If you are naturally pointed to the left, move your right foot back slightly, and your left foot slightly forward, keeping the feet in the same orienta-

tion to each other. If you're pointing above the target, move your right foot closer to your left foot. If you're pointing below the target, move your right foot away from your left foot, again keeping the feet in the same orientation to each other.

Some shooters adjust the fist under the stock to change natural point of aim. This technique can cause strain in the left arm and possibly weaken the hand position. Until you are a more advanced shooter and understand the mechanics, avoid this tactic. If you've adjusted your feet to get your natural point of aim up or down on the target, and your feet are moving extremely close together or far apart, you can adjust your butt plate up or down to help compensate for some of the height disparity. Then you can reposition your feet to a more normal width.

Figure 6.2 Natural point-of-aim adjustments in standing position.

Adjusting Natural Point of Aim in Kneeling Position

The pivot point in kneeling position is the kneeling roll. When you first set up in position, you should be pretty much in the center of the target. This way you can adjust your position right or left and maintain the same kneeling roll placement for the whole match. As in other positions, lift your rifle, place your face on the stock, and take three breaths with your eyes closed. When you open your eyes, see whether you are pointed naturally at the target.

If you are pointed to the right, move your left foot to the left and follow it with your right knee, again keeping that distance parallel (figure 6.3).

(This advice assumes that you are a right handed shooter.) Be sure to rotate the whole kneeling roll as well. Avoid twisting only your ankle on top of the kneeling roll because you could roll to one side. If you are pointed to the left of the target, you'll have to adjust your position to the right. Start by moving your right knee to the right, followed by your left foot. Small changes can be made by simply pointing toe of the left foot slightly, either to the right or the left. If you are pointed too high on the target, try moving your elbow or left foot out slightly or possibly moving your sling or hand stop out one notch. If you are pointing too low on the target, try moving your elbow up on your knee, bringing your left foot in slightly but not beyond perpendicular, or try moving your hand stop in a bit and tightening your sling.

Figure 6.3 Natural point-of-aim adjustments in kneeling position.

Adjusting Natural Point of Aim in Sitting Position

In the sitting position, your rear end is the pivot point. As with the other positions, assume the position and close your eyes while trying to get a steady hold. Take 3 breaths and open your eyes and note where the target is.

If you are pointed to the right, shift your legs over to the left (figure 6.4). Shift in the opposite direction if you are pointed to the left. If you are pointed too high, you can move your feet out. If you are pointed too low, you can try bringing in your feet or repositioning your elbows.

Figure 6.4   Natural point-of-aim adjustments in sitting position.

BREATH CONTROL

Breath control in shooting is a conscious effort of inhaling and exhaling and stopping your breath at a specific point to settle your hold and take a shot on the target (figure 6.5). After your rifle is in place and your face is on the cheek piece, take three slow breaths. In prone or kneeling position, you will see that the muzzle of the rifle crosses over the target at a slight diagonal. Watch this movement and stop your breath when the muzzle is directly over the target. Ideally, the sights should stop on the center of the target when you reach your natual respiratory pause.

Some shooters exhale half to three-quarters of their breath or almost completely exhale to respiratory pause, allowing them to move up onto the target and end their breath in the center. Many do this because they feel a better sense of relaxation when exhaling. Other shooters, including me, inhale about half a breath to move into the middle of the target. The shooters who use breath control this way believe that they can hold on the target longer because their lungs have fresh oxygen in them. But, holding your breath this way may cause you to feel tension in your chest muscles. Try it both ways to see what is more comfortable for you.

By watching your breath control cross the target, you know that you are naturally pointed in the right direction. If after taking several breaths you find it hard to center on the target, that is a clue that your natural point of aim still needs adjustment.

Breath control can set the rhythm for shooting. Many advanced shooters take a certain number of breaths before picking up the rifle, take a certain number of breaths when they settle the rifle, and then hold their breath for only a certain length of time. At first, they consciously take these breaths, but after training a shot plan for a while, the breathing that they do to take a shot becomes automatic.

Most shooters aim for three to eight seconds while holding their breath. If you go beyond eight seconds, you are depriving your brain, eyes, and the rest of your body of oxygen. Longer hold times mean longer recovery times between shots. To avoid this, learn to time yourself. When you get beyond eight seconds, put down the rifle. Beginning shooters often think that they need to pull the trigger every time they put up the rifle, which can lead to extremely long aiming times, or what is called overholding. If you watch advanced shooters, you'll notice that they often put down the rifle instead of shooting a poor shot because an element of the shot process is not correct. This approach allows them to breathe again, refocus the mind, and correct the problem in the hold. Rarely will they try to take a shot just because they put up the rifle. They will do this only when they are very short on match time and have to shoot the shots. Advanced shooters use a specific routine for each shot, and they manage that routine partly through breath control.

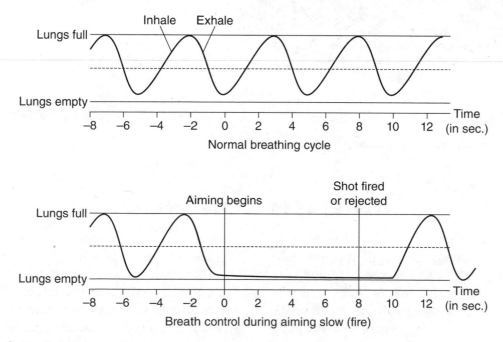

Figure 6.5 Comparison of a normal breathing cycle and breath control while aiming.
Courtesy of the National Rifle Association of America.

HOLD

The hold (figure 6.6) is one of the main elements that make shooting a sport. You work your body and positions to get a smaller hold every time you shoot. Beginning shooters move all over the target with their holds. The more you train, the smaller that movement becomes, creating a smaller hold pattern on the target. You train with your rifle to get a smaller hold. Every day that you shoot, you have to deal with how your body is working and feeling and what kind of hold you can establish that day. The size of your hold can change from day to day, and it can change from the beginning of a match to the end. Most of the work that you put into shooting will be directed at trying to control the hold. Beginning shooters will find it challenging to understand what they are actually seeing while watching the hold. But as you become more skilled, you'll understand when your hold is going to settle, when you should take the shot, and what the hold tells you through the follow-through and resettling on the target after the shot.

The best way to work on hold is to begin with a stable position. You may work for more than a week on establishing a position, and when it feels balanced and stable you can then focus on what your hold looks like through your front sight. If you switch priorities and try to focus only on hold and taking a shot, you will chase yourself in circles. Until your position is stable and consistent, your hold will never be as still as it can be.

After your position is stable, focus on getting the muzzle of the barrel to become as still as possible. You can use many approaches to achieve this, but you will never get away from the fact that you just need to hold your rifle a lot.

One way to start is to place a vertical line on a blank sheet of paper. Create a line that is about as wide as a bull and at least 10 inches (25 cm) long and hang it where you would normally hang a target. First establish your natural point of aim so that it is resting on the line. Now hold on the line for 20 seconds and rest for 30 seconds. Try to build up to practicing this sequence for 20 minutes or longer. While you're holding on the line for 20 seconds, continue to take a couple of breaths every 10 seconds or so and then try to settle your hold on the line while holding your

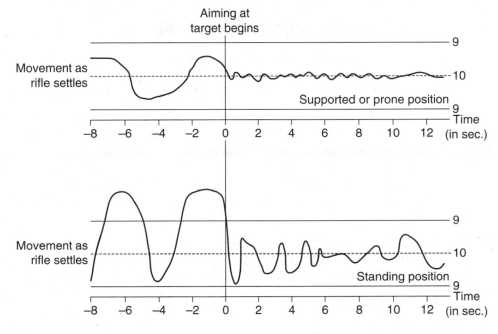

Figure 6.6 Hold.
Courtesy of the National Rifle Association of America.

breath again. For each 20-second cycle, you hold your breath two or three times and watch the muzzle settle on the line.

Why a vertical line? Few positions create a hold that moves up and down. Your focus is trying to eliminate sway, keeping your right and left movement minimal. With a vertical line, you can focus solely on managing that type of movement.

The next exercise is shooting groups. Shoot five-shot groups at one bull and check the center of the group. Click the group into the center of the target and go to the next bull. Your goal is to start getting groups with shots touching and eventually to create just one hole where all the shots go through. You can shoot a whole target this way and get some good training to build endurance and concentration.

If you are at home watching TV or hanging out, you can hold your rifle, aiming at a small dot on the wall or the paper with the vertical line. Doing this builds balance, endurance, and concentration. Practice holding for 20 to 30 seconds to build stamina or work on dry firing.

If for some reason you are having a hard time getting your hold to settle down, spend some time with your eyes closed while holding. Think about how your body feels, identify any tension anywhere, and work on relaxing that area. Check your equipment to be sure that everything is in the right place. You may have to get completely out of position and spend some time stretching. When you get suited up in your gear, be sure that all the buttons and zippers that you need to have buttoned or zipped are indeed as they should be. Many shooters become frustrated when, after they finish shooting, they find that the bottom two buttons on their jackets weren't buttoned, or that their boots came undone, or that they were using the wrong kneeling roll.

On some days, no matter what you do, your hold will be larger than normal. Don't become frustrated. Keep working with the position to see whether you can relax and gain greater control. In a match, you are likely to face a larger and faster-moving hold than you normally do because of the excitement of the day. Seek opportunities to train in that condition to build strategies to manage the situation.

After several weeks of work, your hold will become smaller and you'll have a much better chance of shooting a good shot. Your goal is to shoot a shot that is within your hold, not on the outside of it or even on the edge of it. You want to place your shot right in the middle of the hold pattern that you see, and to do that you need trigger control.

TRIGGER CONTROL

Trigger control (figure 6.7) is the timing used to shoot a good shot within the shooter's hold, ideally in the 10 ring.

Most triggers have two stages. You take up the first stage while you are either taking or releasing your last breath. You take the second stage when you want to shoot the shot. Some triggers have a single stage. These triggers do not have a stopping point after you start to squeeze them. You can back off the trigger and not shoot the shot, but when you've committed to taking the shot, it will go off somewhere between the start of the pull and the end without another stopping point. You need to have a well-established hold to use this type of trigger successfully.

Trigger control and timing the shot go hand in hand. After you take up the first stage and you're ready to squeeze off the shot, you must use timing to take the shot while it's going into the 10 ring versus taking it on the way out of the target center. This element is another factor that makes shooting the sport that it is and why substantial variations occur from shot to shot and from day to day. Timing your shot is similar to playing golf, serving in tennis, bowling, or shooting pool. Before any of those actions take place, the athlete sets body position, establishes proper alignment, and focuses on a specific task. These same characteristics go into good shooting. But we will have good days and bad days, which is why we work so hard. We want to have our good days on the right days.

Timing is a fundamental that you will work on over your entire shooting career. Timing is what

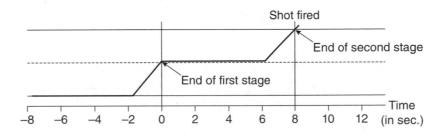

Figure 6.7 Trigger control.
Courtesy of the National Rifle Association of America.

makes shooting fun and frustrating at the same time. You can have a great hold, but until you fire the shot through that hold, no one can tell what a great shooter you really are. You will need training to develop and perfect your timing to the point where you can anticipate when to take the shot as it's moving into the 10 ring. This is another reason to have the right-sized aperture. If the bull is moving in and out of your aperture, you will develop a type of timing in which you snap at the target as it passes by. This bad habit can be tough to overcome. For that reason you should have the right sized aperture. After your hold settles, you can keep the whole hold inside the aperture and have a much better chance to predict when the sights are going to be perfectly lined up on the target because you can see the whole action unfolding right inside it.

To perfect your timing, do the following:

1. Take up your first trigger stage with your last breath.

2. Wait for your hold to settle.

3. Squeeze off the second trigger stage to shoot inside your hold when the sights are moving into the 10 ring.

4. Keep your eyes open for the whole shot. Don't blink as the gun goes off. Doing this may take some practice if you're accustomed to shooting a larger-caliber rifle.

5. Keep your finger on the trigger after the second stage has gone off and keep your finger moving back in the same motion. Avoid letting your finger jump forward after the shot has gone off. Some coaches call this a chicken finger because it's as if the shooter really didn't want to take the shot.

All these elements tie together for smooth and consistent trigger control. But the element that anchors your shot into the 10 ring is the follow-through.

FOLLOW-THROUGH

Follow-through (figure 6.8) is the conscious action to keep your rifle, body, trigger finger, eye, and mind directed toward the center of the target after the rifle has gone off. Having good follow-through means that you are doing nothing to disturb the shot before, during, and after it leaves the barrel. If you can keep looking into the 10 ring after the shot goes off, more likely than not your body and rifle will remain centered on the target, and the shot will follow.

Proper follow-through eliminates jerking. Jerking the trigger is common with beginning shooters because they want to try to catch the target as it passes by. If you consciously stay with the target past the shot, then you're less likely to jerk the trigger because you are already in the location you want to lead to.

Follow-through can also be called the anchor of the shot because if you are doing everything in your shot process to stay in the center past the shot, then you will avoid taking shots that won't let you achieve this. Instead of taking poor-quality shots, you'll put the gun down before they have the chance to subtract from your score.

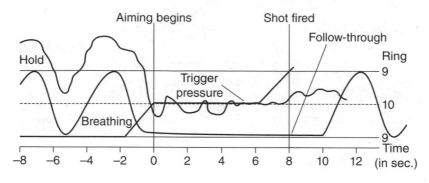

Figure 6.8 Follow-through.
Courtesy of the National Rifle Association of America.

During follow-through you'll also have the opportunity to read your recoil. Recoil is the reaction that the rifle has after a shot is fired. Recoil is a more significant factor in small bore because the rifle actually moves up and down when the ammunition is fired. Because air rifle shooting doesn't involve gunpowder, the rifle has the potential to stay right in the center of the target after the shot goes off. But if the rifle does move right or left during follow-through and stays there for some reason, that is another clue that your natural point of aim may be off because the rifle wants to resettle naturally in a different location. Taking enough time in follow-through to see what the rifle does is critical to identifying any weak areas of the position or hold, and to anchor yourself mentally into the 10 ring past the shot. Seeing this critical information is essential to good performance and is the reason for keeping your eyes open.

For many beginning shooters, looking at the shot in the scope is the most exciting aspect of the sport. Sometimes this desire interferes with follow-through. I've seen some shooters trying to look at their score almost before the pellet could have hit the target. This type of habit seriously cuts into any kind of follow-through after the shot. If you try to use the scope as the sole source of shooting excitement, remember to take some extra time to follow through, watch for any recoil, and call your shot.

SHOT CALLING

Before you look into your scope, think about what you saw in your hold, how you timed the shot, and what happened with the rifle if it recoiled to another location during follow-through. Use all this information to predict where your shot should be on the target. Do this after each shot before you look into your scope. Identify what you saw and felt during the shot process. After you have the location of the shot in your mind, look into the scope to verify what actually happened. You should call your shot before you look into the scope because if the shot is not in the location where you believe it should be, you know that you need to adjust your sights. If you just take it for granted that the location of the shot is where you took it, then you won't click your sights soon enough and will continue to shoot in this area, which is probably not over the 10 ring.

Calling shots takes practice and experience. In the beginning, you're trying to identify exactly where the sights were pointing and go with that information. But as you progress, you'll add the anticipation of going into the 10 ring, the timing of the hold movements, the speed of the hold, and the place the sights ended up after the shot. If you are shooting outside, you'll add the wind into the formula when calling your shot. Don't worry that many elements are involved. With practice, you'll continue to pick up on more of the information available to you as it becomes more familiar.

Use the information that you learned from the previous shot to make decisions about your plan of attack for your next shot. Some of the information that you'll use includes

- putting the gun correctly into place,
- positioning your face on the cheek piece,
- identifying and relaxing any tension,
- stopping your breath for the hold,
- getting your hold to settle down,
- timing the hold with correct anticipation and reaction to seeing the sights and target line up,

- following through after the shot, and
- checking that recoil remains over the center of the target.

These are the main elements to pay attention to. As you progress in the sport, some of the elements will become more important and others less important to your particular style of shooting. Just be sure not to take any of them for granted until your shot plans are fully developed and you know the areas that you need to focus on.

A SHOT FROM EACH POSITION

When you learn the shooting positions, you will find that you like to shoot some positions more than you do others. Some shooters prefer prone position because it is the most stable position. Some like standing position because it requires the best timing and intuition. Other like kneeling position because they believe that it is the most technical. Ideally, you will enjoy shooting from all the positions and work to master each one.

Because each position has a unique structure and support system, your hold will look different in each one. Prone position and kneeling position feature the support of the left elbow on either the ground or the knee, so the movement up and down is minimal. The main up-and-down movement comes from the breaths that you take before you begin to hold. Standing position does provide the support of the elbow on the hip area, but it has to cover a larger hold area. Because of these differences, you will likely take shots differently from each position.

Prone position. Prone is the most stable position, so it should produce the smallest hold. You can take shots sooner from prone position because the hold is over the 10 ring for a longer time, allowing successful shots to be taken. Although you will quickly develop a 10-ring hold, timing is still critical in prone position. You are now dealing with a hold that is literally sitting on

the dot. Because it's already over the dot, if you move off the dot by half the width of the pellet, you will shoot a 9. Follow-through is important so that you know the timing of your hold will stay over the 10 ring past the shot and not move away from it, because that's really the only direction that it can go. Getting closer to the 10 ring is tough when you are already sitting on top of it.

Standing position. From standing position, the hold can move around the target easily, so you must focus on your hold to get it as steady as possible. Of the three positions, standing may have the longest hold before the shot goes off because you need to watch the hold for a while to anticipate when it's either going to settle on the 10 ring or slow down enough to shoot the shot as it's going into the 10 ring. Trigger control and timing are critical. You need to be ready to take the shot when the correct sight picture presents itself. If the first stage still needs to be taken and the hold settles on the bull, you've missed your opportunity to take that shot. If you try to go through the first and second trigger stages while the rifle is completely settled, it will already be moving out of the 10 ring by the time the shot goes off. Follow-through in standing is also longer than it is in the other positions because you want to gather as much information as possible after the shot by reading the recoil or where the rifle moves after the shot.

Kneeling position. Kneeling should be the second most stable position. Because of the sling and the elbow placement on the knee, you'll likely see some pulse in your hold. Keep trying to adjust your position and your equipment to reduce the pulse. The hold usually moves from left to right if it's going to move at all. Be sure to get the center of that movement over the center of your bull. With trigger control and timing, try to get into a rhythm so that you are taking the shot at the same time during your hold each time. If a moment occurs when the sights consistently settle on the bull, wait for that time to come and then shoot. If you consistently have a pulse that moves across the bull, establish a pattern of taking the shot when it comes back to one specific side. Set up your natural point of aim so that the stopping point is over the bull. You want to time the shot as it is moving into that location ahead of the time when it stops.

Sitting position. The hold for sitting most likely will have some slight right and left movement. Remember, because both elbows are anchored, you'll have less side-to-side movement than you do in kneeling, and you control the up-and-down movement through properly holding your breath. You can develop a small hold in sitting if you have time to train it. Some pulse may be present, so double-check to see whether you can relieve any of it by opening your jacket and pants or adjusting your sling. If the pulse is still present, follow the trigger control instructions for kneeling by adjusting your NPA so that the resting point of the pulse is over the center of the target.

Using various shooting strategies for each position is fun and challenging. You will have to try several approaches and timing techniques to see what works best and helps you perform consistently.

How your body feels on a particular day will also dictate what kind of approach you'll take for your shots. If you feel tight and your hold is not as good as you'd like, you may take shots faster to get them off before the hold breaks down. If you have an incredibly good hold, you may become caught up in admiring it and then overhold your shot. Admiring your hold is fine, but be sure to get your shot off with a follow-through that continues to stay in the 10 ring. Be ready for what the day brings, and learn as much about controlling your body and mind as you can. That's the great part about shooting—what you learn today can be applied to tomorrow and your scores will continue to improve.

SUCCESS SUMMARY OF TAKING THE SHOT

Through this step, you learned to take a shot (finally). You put together all the parts of a good shot with practice and discipline and made each shot a fluid action. You should learn to break down the elements and identify what goes into each part of the shot process. That way when something breaks down, you'll be able to identify it faster and have more success at fixing it before it hurts your performance.

In the next step, you'll get a good idea about what it takes to prepare for a match, who to contact, and how to build a competition routine that makes the most of your time. The information will account for many of the variables that determine whether you're prepared and will have a positive performance. Keep working on your positions, hold, and the timing of your shots because we are getting ready to go into competition.

Before Taking the Next Step

Before moving on to step 7, Preparing for Competition, evaluate what you have learned to this point. Answer each of the following questions honestly. If you can answer all nine questions, you are ready to move on to the next step.

1. Can you establish your natural point of aim in each position?
2. Do you know what the pivot points are in each position?
3. Can you adjust each position higher or lower?
4. Have you established what kind of a breath gives you the best hold and how full or empty your lungs are when you shoot?
5. Do you know how long you can have a good hold on the target and when it starts to break down?
6. Have you tested your ability to shoot inside your hold?
7. What does it mean if your shots are going wider than your hold?
8. Why is follow-through important?
9. What are the elements that you look at when calling your shot?

Preparing for Competition

Shooting is an amazing sport because everyone competes on an equal playing field. For men and women, for people short and tall, for those intense and easy going, shooting can be a sport to take you all the way to the Olympic Games.

Most shooters get their start from humble beginnings. They may take their first shots in the backyard (providing it's a safe range space, of course), out hunting in the woods, or on a range at a fair or youth event. After those first few shots, some are hooked and want to become proficient at hitting the target every time. From this simple start, the rifle becomes a piece of sporting equipment used to show proficiency at marksmanship.

Shooters find the most joy by shooting a score higher than they ever have before. This sport measures progress at the shooter's own pace. You certainly can compare your scores with those of other shooters, but the reward of satisfaction comes down to shooting better than you have in the past. And if that beats the other competitors, all the better. Here are some important topics to cover to help you get ready for competition.

LEARN THE RULES

Eight organizations sanction three-position air rifle matches. The National Rifle Association (NRA) is one of those organizations, and it has its own rule book, *NRA Precision Air Rifle Position Rules*. If the ranges in your area shoot NRA-sanctioned matches, participate in as many matches as you can. You can order an NRA rule book from the NRA at their Web site. See Additional Resources (page 163) for contact information.

To find a list of matches in your area, go to the NRA's competitions Web site and navigate through the information provided. See Additional Resources for Web site information.

You may discover that some matches are not too distant from you, and you may want to make the drive and compete. Contact the match director by using the phone number or e-mail listed and let him or her know that you want to come and shoot. Hosting organizations use initials to describe the matches that they host. IN means international air rifle, which consists of 60 shots from the standing position for men and 40 shots from the standing position for women. PRE means precision air rifle, which consists of 20 shots from the prone position, 20 shots from the standing position, and 20 shots from the kneeling position. Some organizations shoot only 10 shots per position, so check the match program to see how they plan their course of fire. SPT means sporter air rifle, a beginning rifle used by many junior programs. NRA sporter rifle events have their own rule book called *NRA Sporter Air Rifle Position Rules*. If that is what is shot in your area, you'll want to get a copy of that rule book as well. Rule books cost $2.50 each and are usually valid for at least two years.

The other rule book that you may need is the *National Standard Three-Position Air Rifle Rules*, published by the National Three-Position Air Rifle Council. The organizations that use this rule book in competition include the American Legion; the Boy Scouts of America–Venturing; the Civilian Marksmanship Program (CMP); the Daisy/U.S. Jaycees Shooter Education Program; the National 4-H Shooting Sports; the U.S. Army Marksmanship Unit; USA Shooting; and the Air Force, Army, Marine Corps, and Navy JROTC Commands. This rule book includes rules for both sporter and precision air rifle shooting matches. Rule books cost $2.00. To obtain a copy, contact the National Three-Position Air Rifle Council. See Additional Resources (page 163) for contact information.

You can also view and download the rules from the CMP at their Web site. See Additional Resources (page 163) for more information.

Shooters usually first get involved in structured shooting with one of these organizations. After you get your feet on the ground and understand how the sport works, find other opportunities to shoot in your area. You may find additional ranges nearby where you can join a junior club (and have more practice time) or at least compete in the matches that they host. You can stay with the program that you start with, but to gain additional experience and find other shooting opportunities, you need to get involved with other programs in your area. You may get to shoot silhouette, high power, black powder, cowboy, or even pistol, and have even more fun with the shooting sports.

After you've decided to shoot in a match, follow these guidelines to participate.

SIGN UP

Contact the match director by e-mail or phone to let him or her know that you are coming and to get on a relay. One group of shooters on the line at the same time is called a relay. A match usually has two or more relays of shooters because a range is usually not large enough to hold all the shooters who want to shoot at the same time. Shooters are divided and scheduled to shoot at different times, and each of these times designates a different relay. Ask what relay times are still available and see which one works best for your schedule. In some matches, you won't have a choice on the time that you shoot and the match director will let you know what time the match starts. Ask for a match program or the match information sheet. Sometimes you can print these from the Internet, or the match director will send one to you. The match program provides all the information you need to know about the competition. It may include the following:

- Name of the match
- Dates
- Location
- Type of match—includes events and other information such as whether the match is a preliminary tryout, sectional, U.S. team tryout, and so on.
- Sponsors
- Housing availability—a list of available hotels; if the match is at the Olympic Training Center or other national-level competition such as Camp Perry, housing may be provided.
- Squadding, a list of relay times—you may or may not have your choice of time.

- Finals—some matches have these at the end of the competition as the Olympics does.

- Classification system—USA Shooting and the NRA each have their own classification system. This system is used so that you compete in a category with shooters similar to your ability level and experience. Although everyone competes together, you have the chance to win in your category and you don't have to compete against advanced shooters. Of course, after you become a master, you will be competing against the best shooters.

- Jury—group of people who decide on challenges, protests, and potential rules violations.

- Eligibility—some matches require that you belong to a particular organization such as USA Shooting. This requirement is for liability purposes and for tracking your progress in classification.

- Targets—describes the type of targets shot in the match. You may have a target with 5- or 10-record bulls on it if you're shooting NRA targets. You may have a single-bull target if you're shooting a USA Shooting match. And if you're lucky, you may be shooting on electronic targets, which is like shooting at a single-bull target the whole match with monitor feedback.

- Shooting mats—some ranges provide shooting mats so that you don't need to haul yours with you.

- Time limits—listed for each kind of match that is shot in the competition.

- Sighting shots—a reminder that you can take unlimited sighting shots before going for record, but that you cannot take additional sighting shots after you start record fire.

- Scoring challenges—usually a $1 or $2 fee is charged if you want to challenge a score. If you are given a value of 9 on a shot but you think that it should be a 10,

you have the right to challenge the score. If it ends up that you were correct, you get your challenge fee back. If the scorers were correct, they keep your fee. A small fee is charged so competitors don't challenge every shot.

- Match schedule—a list of all the matches available to shoot.

- Awards—tells you what type of awards are given: cash, merchandise, medals, or trophies.

- Fees—lets you know the cost of each match and whether a package entry fee (discount for two or more matches) is available, whether a deposit is required, and whether fees need to be submitted ahead of time.

- Entry form—fill out the attached form and send it ahead of time so that they know to squad you. Pay attention to when you need to return the form and whether you need to send a deposit.

- Practice schedule—many big matches have a practice day ahead of the match and make other practice times available after the conclusion of shooting on match days.

- Competition schedule—lists all the matches and their dates, times, and ranges if shot on multiple days and ranges.

- Address—where to send entries and how to contact the match director.

- Figure 7.1 shows a sample match program similar to one that you might receive when you enter a competition.

The preceding list contains a lot of information, but before you arrive at a match you want to be sure that you understand the schedule for the day. This includes when you'll be shooting each match, when you should eat, when you'll be finished, and all the other nuggets of information that will help you stay ahead of the game. To do this effectively, you need to develop a prematch routine.

Official Match Program

RIFLE CLASSIC

Montgomery Bell Academy

The 14th annual MBA Rifle Classic will be held in Nashville, Tennessee, over the weekend of October 17 through 19. The Rifle Classic, which provides season opening competition for high school teams, is the largest high school sponsored shooting event in the U.S. It includes two separate competitions:

Position Air Rifle Tournament. This is the main event. It is limited to teams and individuals representing high schools. The tournament is sanctioned by:

- Tennessee Secondary Schools Athletic Association and the Georgia High School Association.
- USA Shooting to permit scores fired to be recognized as national records.
- Civilian Marksmanship Program as a CMP Cup Match. Competitors may earn EIC credit points for the Junior Distinguished Badge.

Open International Standing Match. This 40-shot, Sunday-morning event allows teams staying overnight to compete in another match before heading home. It is open to both high school and club teams.

A major goal of the Classic is to showcase talented high school athletes for college rifle coaches. Many college rifle coaches attend the competition to observe the shooting and to visit with the high school coaches. The Official Results Bulletins are designed to be handy prospecting tools for college coaches.

Competitors and the general public are invited to enjoy the following:

Position Rifle Clinics. The Army Marksmanship Unit from Fort Benning, Georgia, will conduct the following rifle clinics:

Friday:

Standing 3:00-4:15

Prone and Kneeling 5:00-6:15

Eliminating the "Oops Factor!" 7:00-8:15

Saturday:

Standing 9:00-10:15

Prone and Kneeling 11:00-12:15

Eliminating the "Oops Factor!" 1:00-2:15

Road to the Olympics 3:00-4:15

Champion's Choice, the largest mail-order competitive shooting supply house in the U.S., operates an equipment display and sales operation in Frist Hall from 3:00 to 9:00 p.m. on Friday and 9:00 a.m. to 4:30 p.m. on Saturday. This display is highly popular with both athletes and coaches.

Finals Competition and Award Ceremony. These events start at 7:00 p.m. Saturday evening and will be completed by 9:00 p.m. Finals will open with the Sporter Class followed by Precision. Individual medals will be presented at the conclusion of each finals. The evening concludes with the presentation of team awards.

Figure 7.1 Sample match program.
Courtesy of the Montgomery Bell Academy.

POSITION AIR RIFLE TOURNAMENT
FRIDAY AND SATURDAY, OCTOBER 17 AND 18

Eligibility: Entry is limited to shooting athletes who are enrolled in the high school they represent and are students in good standing. Entries from Georgia must be students in good standing at a GHSA affiliated high school. All entries must represent a high school; no club, collegiate, or pickup entries are allowed.

Classes: There are two classes for competition and awards—Sporter and Precision.

Course of Fire: Position air rifle 3 × 20 (National Standard Rules), 20 shots each prone, standing, and kneeling fired in this order. The top eight competitors in each class fire a 10 shot finals Saturday evening to determine the medal winners.

Conduct of Match: The match will be conducted in accordance with the current National Standard Three-Position Air Rifle Rules. All entrants will compete as individuals. Six AR-5/10 targets are hung at the start of a relay. Positions will be fired in timed stages (30 minutes for prone, 40 minutes for standing and 30 minutes for kneeling).

Team Match: There is a four-member paper team match using scores from the individual competition. Mixed teams will compete in the highest class of any team member. Team score cards must be presented to the Range Officer before any team member fires a record shot.

Relay Times:

Friday:

Relay 1 (1:30 to 4:00 p.m.)

Relay 2 (4:00 to 6:30 p.m.)

Relay 3 (6:30 to 9:00 p.m.)

Saturday:

Relay 4 (8:00 to 10:30 a.m.)

Relay 5 (10:30 to 1:00 p.m.)

Relay 6 (1:00 to 3:30 p.m.)

Relay 7 (3:30 to 6:00 p.m.). No sporters may fire on Relay 7.

Finals: The finals for the top eight shooters in the Sporter Class will start at 7:00 p.m. followed by the Precision finals. All competitors are encouraged to attend the finals and the award ceremonies which follow.

Awards: Gold, silver, and bronze medals will be awarded in the 60 shot individual aggregate plus finals for each class. Trophy plaques will be awarded to the top three teams in each class along with medals for firing team members and coach. Individuals and all team members must be present at the Awards Ceremony following the finals to receive their awards and to be photographed or they will forfeit their awards. The coach and all firing members of the team winning the Deneke Trophy must be present at the Awards Ceremony or the award is forfeied.

Entry Fees: The entry fee is $25 for each individual competitor. There is no additional fee for team entries.

Squadding: Teams will be assigned relays based on their entry request and availability when their entry request is received.

Assignment of Firing Lanes: Firing lanes will be assigned by drawing on Thursday before the Classic. Lane assignments will be posted on each range and in Frist Hall.

Report Time: Teams should arrive at MBA not later than one hour before the start of their relay. Shooters should report to the ready line 10 minutes before their relay. They will be called to move onto the firing line at their relay time. There will be a 10-minute preparation period. Nashville is in the Central Time Zone.

Challenge Period: Targets should be ready for challenge approximately one hour after end of a relay. The start of the challenge period will be announced in the Frist Hall cafeteria. The Challenge Office will be in the Gibbs Room (down the hall from the cafeteria).

Competitor I.D. Panels: A souvenir Rifle Classic I.D. Panel will be provided for each competitor. It is requested that an I.D. Panel be worn on the back of each competitor. This will make it easier for college coaches to identify shooters and the teams they represent.

Rifle Classic Decals: Each competitor will receive an unique tournament decal as a memento. The decals have become collector's items that are applied to rifle stocks and gun cases.

(continued)

(continued)

ACE HARDWARE COACHES MATCH
SATURDAY, OCTOBER 18 AT 6:15 P.M.
(Small Gym)

The Coaches Match is a no-entry fee fun match for the head coach of each school with a team entered in the 3P team competition. The match will be 10 shots standing using the finals course of fire.

Ace Hardware gift certificates are awarded to the winner, 2nd, and 3rd place ($75, $50, $25) along with gold, silver, and bronze trophy hammers.

OPEN INTERNATIONAL STANDING MATCH
SUNDAY, OCTOBER 19

Eligibility: This match is open to high school and club teams. Home school athletes may enter. Entries must be age 19 or under. Entry is limited to 114 competitors.

Classes: There are two classes—Sporter and Precision.

Course of Fire: Forty shots standing air rifle (National Standard Rules) fired in two stages.

Conduct of Match: All entrants will compete as individuals (no coaching). Two AR-5/10 targets will be mounted with 40 minutes to fire 20 record shots. Targets will be exchanged and shooters will have 40 minutes to fire their second 20 shots for record.

Team Match: There is a four-member paper team match using scores from the individual competition; mixed teams (precision/sporter) will compete in the Precision Category. Team score cards must be turned in to the Range Officer before any team member fires a record shot.

Relay Times:

Relay 1 (8:00 to 9:45 a.m.)

Relay 2 (9:45 to 11:30 a.m.)

Entry Fees: The entry fee is $10 for each individual competitor. There is no additional fee for the four-member team event. The team event is a paper match.

MBA RIFLE CLASSIC

(Please print or type)

TO: Tournament sponsor

FROM: _____   CONTACT INFORMATION: _____

Coach _____   Home: (   ) _____

School _____   Work: (   ) _____

Address _____   FAX: (   ) _____

_____   e-mail _____

The above information will appear in the Official Results Bulletin that will be sent to college rifle coaches.

1. **Position Air Rifle Tournament.** We wish to make the following entries:

    Individual entries: _____ Shooters × $25 = $ _____ No additional charge for team entries.

    Enter 1, 2, or 3 in boxes to show relay preference:

    ❑ Relay 1 (1:30–4 Friday)   ❑ Relay 2 (4–6:30 Friday)

    ❑ Relay 3 (6:30–9 Friday)   ❑ Relay 4 (8–10:30 Saturday)

    ❑ Relay 5 (10:30–1 Saturday)   ❑ Relay 6 (1–3:30 Saturday)

        ❑ Relay 7 (3:30–6 Saturday, Limited to Precision Only)

    Indicate range preference: Small gym _____ Big gym _____ No preference _____

    Estimate the number of competitors you will have in each class: Sporter _____ Precision _____

2. **Open International Standing Match.** We wish to make the following entries:

    Individual entries: _____ Shooters × $10 = $ _____ No additional charge for team entries.

Relay preference:

        ❑ Relay 1 (8–9:45 a.m. Sunday)   ❑ Relay 2 (9:45–11:30 a.m. Sunday)

3. Total entry fees for the above matches are enclosed in the form of a check payable to MBA:

    Total amount enclosed $ _____

I understand that 3P award recipients are required to attend the Award Ceremony or forfeit awards.

Signature _____ Date _____

PREMATCH ROUTINE

Advanced shooters use a prematch routine (figure 7.2) to account for all the things that they need to take care of so that they are ready to shoot when the range officer says, "Commence fire" or "Start." Some shooters begin their routines the minute they wake up. They determine the schedule down to the minute because they know that they'll need a certain amount of time to feel ready for the match. Some shooters have a three-hour rule, which corresponds to the amount of time that they need between waking up and shooting the first shot down range. The routine gives them enough time to get out of bed, shower, eat a good breakfast, and stretch before they even head to the range. To a beginning shooter, that length of time may seem extreme, but you should be sure to allow enough time to be ready, rested, and focused for shooting. Trying to wake up, eat, get to the range, and throw your gear together in an hour is probably cutting it a little close.

Eating

As you compete, you'll notice that eating too close to the time that you shoot will cause an increase in the volume of your pulse. In addition, your stomach may feel uncomfortable because it's trying to digest your meal and control those unexpected butterflies. Timing the first meal of the day is important so that you have a chance to digest it before the match and have the right amount and kind of calories to sustain you through the competition. Although you are mostly motionless in shooting matches, your body and brain are working as they do when you are taking an important test or performing a music solo. A lot of energy goes into concentrating, dealing with stress, and managing mind over matter in the art of shooting. Most shooters are exhausted after a match, even though they hadn't moved their bodies much at all. Here are some suggestions for foods to eat before matches.

Two to three hours before competition: Try a bagel with low-fat cream cheese, lean meat on whole-grain bread, a baked potato, whole-grain cereal with low-fat milk, an energy bar, an apple with peanut butter, pasta, fresh fruit or vegetable, other whole-grain items, low-fat yogurt, or cottage cheese.

You can gauge when to eat by how fast you digest food. Athletes who have a high metabolism and eat three to four hours before competition may be completely depleted and out of energy by the end of a match. Eating multiple small meals closer to competition makes sense for them because they can digest the food before they start. If you have a slower metabolism and feel as if you still have something in your stomach after three hours (and you'll know this when you're shooting prone), then you know to adjust the time when you eat or what you eat.

One hour before competition and snacks between matches: Consume fresh fruit or vegetables, vegetable juice, whole-grain items such as crackers, or other easily digestible foods that are complex carbohydrate.

Because matches can last two hours or longer, you may need some energy to sustain you through the competition. Pick items that you have eaten before or during practice that you know don't have a negative effect. You don't want to feel full, and you don't want a spike in blood sugar that can cause you to become jittery and increase your pulse. The best advice is to try healthy items before you practice and see what kind of plan you need to put into place to have energy for the match. The goal is to avoid feeling too full when you shoot but not becoming run down by the end of the match.

Avoid anything with caffeine and anything with a lot of simple carbohydrate (sugar) such as candy, soda, or doughnuts. These foods will spike your blood sugar and cause you to run out of energy sooner than you will if you had eaten a bagel an hour earlier. Caffeine will make you jittery and increase your hold movements.

Prematch Timeline and Checklist

6:00 a.m.   Wake up and shower.

6:30 a.m.   Eat breakfast of whole-wheat bagel with peanut butter, fruit, low-fat yogurt, and juice.

6:45 a.m.   Do stretching, relaxing, and imagery.

7:00 a.m.   Load the car and drive to the range.

7:15 a.m.   Arrive at the range

7:20 a.m.   Check in at the stat office, pay entry fees, and pick up the shooter's packet.

7:30 a.m.   Start setting up rifle and gear.

7:50 a.m.   When relay 1 is called to the line, move gear to the firing point.

7:55 a.m.   Set up mat, scope, tools, and all other equipment needed for the whole match. Lie down on the mat to set the scope correctly, put all other items in the correct place for the match, and get a feel for where prone angle will be. Bring in the rifle, check it again for settings, and set it beside the mat.

8:10 a.m.   Put in ear plugs, do some light stretching, relax, and focus.

8:18 a.m.   Put on jacket, pants, and boots and get into position without the rifle. Check gear to see that it is in the right starting place for prone position.

8:20 a.m.   Start prep period. Hook up the rifle. Check that everything is in place and put the rifle in position. Check natural head placement, looking straight through sights. Check that the gun feels balanced and wants to stay in position. Establish natural point of aim. Close eyes and breathe to help position settle naturally. Open eyes and see where the rifle is pointing. Adjust position if needed. Keep doing this until naturally pointed at the center of the target and can repeat process a couple of times without any corrections. Watch hold. Make hold as small as possible by relaxing and letting the sling do the work in prone and kneeling position and letting bone structure do the work in standing position. Settle hold as much as possible. Double-check natural point of aim. Dry fire. Focus on squeezing off the shot inside hold. Dry fire again to work on timing and follow-through. Check natural point of aim one more time.

8:30 a.m.   Start is announced.

Figure 7.2 Example of a prematch routine.

Arriving at the Range

Plan to arrive about an hour before the start of your match. If you're not sure of the location or traffic, add some extra driving time into your plan. You want to arrive with plenty of time to sign in and set up.

Signing In

When you arrive, go into the match and see where the range director has set up the stat office. This could be a table right in the middle of the staging area, a back room on the range, or a location in another building. After you find the stat office, check in and pick up your shooter's packet, if one is available. A shooter's packet may contain your competitor number, any changes to the match, the point number that you're shooting on, and possibly another information card to complete. Some matches don't have shooter packets and simply list important information on a sheet of paper posted on the wall. Be ready for anything!

Complying With Equipment Control

Some advanced matches such as the Junior Olympics, NCAA National Championships, and some preliminary tryout matches use what is called equipment control. Equipment control is a place at the range where you go before the match starts to have your gun, jacket, pants, boots, sling, and glove checked by an official to make sure that they fall within the rules. Add additional time to your prematch routine if equipment control is listed in the match program.

At large matches such as World Cups and important international matches, equipment control is a standard practice. Going through it is useful because you then know that all your gear meets the rules. Equipment control is rarely practiced in local matches, so don't expect it until you shoot in larger competitions. At local matches, line officers will inspect your equipment by sight when you are on the line to check whether anything is way outside the rules.

Setting Up

Usually a staging area is located behind the range. Few line officers will allow you out on your point an hour before the match to set up, so you'll have to do most of your setting up before you get out on the line. In the staging area, find a place to set down your gear. Start putting together your gun as soon as you can after checking in if you are allowed to do so in that area. You may have to wait until you get out on the line to set up your gun. This rule can vary from range to range. If you can put together your rifle in the setup area, check all your pieces including your sights and aperture, to be sure that they are tight and in the right place. If something is wrong with your gun, such as a broken cheek piece or a stripped screw, you still have enough time to correct the problem before the match. If a problem is going to take a while to fix, you can ask the match director to resquad you (if possible) so that you can shoot at a later time. If you wait until the last minute to set up your gun during prep period and something is wrong, you will have no time to fix it and will have to shoot with a broken gun or start the match late. At that point, resquadding you probably won't be possible.

After you set up your rifle, put it back in your hard rifle case for protection or put it on the bipod and set it aside and out of the way. A gun rack may be available. A gun rack is another way to keep your gun off the ground and prevent it from being bumped or knocked over.

If you're shooting paper targets, set up your scope so that it is ready for the prone position (if you're shooting a 3 × 20). You can also set up your offhand stand so that it is ready for the standing position. You can put on some of your shooting clothes, such as your tights, sweats, or shooting sweater, but hold off on your jacket, pants, and boots until you are on the line.

Warming Up

Now that some of the larger items are set up and the rest of the equipment is ready to go, focus on a physical warm-up. Many shooters like to stretch before they shoot. You should decide when to stretch by considering what kind of athlete you are. Some highly trained athletes may have a large rise in pulse right after they stretch, because stretching is a signal to the body that it is getting ready for physical activity. To avoid having this kind of rise in pulse, which would affect their holds, they do most of their stretching an hour or more before they shoot (possibly even before they leave for the range) and do a little more before prep period. If you don't experience this change in pulse, you can stretch anytime before the match. Complete your stretching before the prep period, however, so that you can spend that time getting your position warmed up and ready.

If you've never stretched before, get additional information about stretching before you begin. A good resource is the book *Stretching* by Bob Anderson (2002, Shelter Publications). If you feel pain while stretching, stop the stretch and have the pain checked out. Stretching will slowly pull on the muscles, but you shouldn't do it to the point of pain. Stretching before a match can help you relax and provide you with better body awareness during your shooting. When something starts to tense up, you'll be able to pinpoint it and restretch that area if needed. Stretching should also help you stay more relaxed and in control of your body over the course of the day.

To help with the stretch, inhale deeply and then slowly stretch into position as you exhale. While in the stretch, breathe slowly and hold the stretch for 10 to 30 seconds. You should feel tension, but not pain, in the muscle that you are stretching. Don't bounce while holding the stretch in an attempt to stretch farther. Let the muscle relax and stretch as you hold the position.

Stretches can be done from various positions. Lie on your back and perform a simple elongation stretch for the whole body, raising your arms overhead and stretching your arms and feet in opposite directions (figure 7.3a). Bring the knees to the chest to stretch the back and hips (figure 7.3b). Lie on your side and perform a quadriceps stretch (figure 7.3c). Sit up and stretch the quadriceps, hips, and hamstrings with a bent-leg stretch (figure 7.3d). Get on your hands and knees and do a cat stretch for the back, first arching up (figure 7.3e), then down (figure 7.3f). Bring your arms forward and your chest down to stretch your sides and arms (figure 7.3g). Stretch the Achilles tendon and ankle (figure 7.3h), and stretch the leg and hip from a lunge position (figure 7.3i). Sit up tall. Bring an elbow across your chest to stretch the shoulder (figure 7.3j) and then lift the elbow behind your head. Stand to finish stretching. You may find it more comfortable to remove your shooting sweater. Clasp your hands behind your back (figure 7.3k). Lift the hands overhead and bend to the side (figure 7.3l). Finish by stretching the neck (figure 7.3m).

You may see shooters wearing headphones or being quiet and getting into their own world while they stretch or get ready for the match. They use this specific part of their prematch routine to prepare their minds for competition. Some shooters need to get psyched up, but most need to feel calm and relaxed. They take this time to get their minds and bodies into performance mode. You need to know how much time you require either to relax or to get psyched up so that you can set aside the necessary time in your prematch routine to accomplish it.

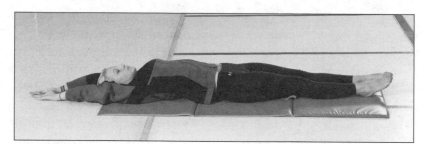

(a) full-body elongation

(b) knees to chest

(c) quadriceps stretch

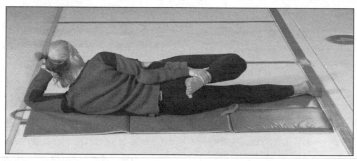

(d) bent-leg stretch

(e) cat stretch, arching back up

(f) cat stretch, arching back down

Figure 7.3 Sample stretching routine.

(continued)

(g) arms forward, chest down

(h) Achilles and ankle stretch

(i) lunge stretch

(j) elbow across chest

(k) hands behind back

(l) side bend

(m) neck stretch

Figure 7.3 *(continued)*

"Relay 1, Shooters to the Line"

The line officer makes this call from the range, which is your signal to pick up your gear and head to your firing point. When you first arrive, ask how much time you will have on the line before the prep period. What you want to know is how much time you'll have on your point before you can pick up your rifle in prep. Sometimes you'll have 30 or 40 minutes, and sometimes you'll have only 20. For that reason, you need to have just about everything ready for the match before you even get out on the firing line.

Go out with your equipment bag and set up your mat and scope first. Get your pellets ready (but do not open them) and set out all the tools you may need throughout the match on your mat. Set out your jacket, pants, and boots so that they are ready to be put on. Use a chair if one is available. After all the items are in place, go back and get your rifle. Many rifles are knocked over on the firing line while shooters assemble and move all the rest of their gear. Remember that after you put your rifle on the firing line, you won't be allowed to pick it up or even touch it again until the prep period is called. This rule is in place because people may be down range setting up targets or coming around to check on gear and shooters, so handling rifles is unsafe.

Finish setting up the rest of your equipment. Place your timer, set up your offhand stand to the back of your point so that it is ready to go, put your glove and sling out on the mat, get your visor ready (if you use one), and finally get your journal out and ready in case you need it for reference, guidance, or reassurance.

If you have some extra time before the prep period, stretch, continue to go through your mental warm-up, listen to music, or just look around the range to familiarize yourself with the lighting. Identify any external features that are new to you such as noise, the kind of target carriers in use, electronic monitors, or other items that you may need to learn to work before the match starts. Usually an explanation or demonstration is provided, but not always.

As the last few minutes before the prep period tick down, put on your jacket, pants, boots, sling, and glove. You want to be ready when the prep period is announced.

"Your 10-Minute Preparation Period Begins Now"

After this announcement is made, you are allowed to pick up your rifle and get into position. You want to get into position as soon as you can. This is not the time to assemble your gun, move your equipment, or stretch. This is the time to establish and settle your position and make sure that you feel solid and ready. If for some reason your position does not feel good, if you have movement or pain, you will have time to make changes and establish a better position.

Some shooters like to practice standing position without a jacket on. They do some holding exercises while wearing just a sweater, pants, and boots to warm up their back and leg muscles. Because they can pick up their guns only during the prep period (this example is for a 60-shot standing match), they have a specific timeline in which to warm up, put on their jackets, reestablish position, dry-fire, and focus for the start of the match. Many do this before they shoot standing position in a 3 × 20 match, and they need to add that into their match plan as well for timing.

You will need some time to warm up and feel settled in your position. Your position will feel different 5 or even 10 minutes after you assume it. You want to feel steady and solid when you hear "Start" or "Commence fire" to begin the match. You want to triple-check your natural point of aim and dry-fire as well. Doing this moves your focus away from verifying that everything is correct physically and into seeing what your body gives you that day as far as hold goes. Then work the hold to settle it down. After the hold settles and starts to look consistent, work on timing with your dry firing. Before the match even begins, you'll want to feel that you are centered, focused, and have the timing down to shoot 10s all day.

As you can see, even if you are ready to shoot as soon as you get to your firing point, you must account for many elements in those last 10 minutes of the prep period to focus for the match.

If you flop down 9 minutes into the prep period and take aim, you won't have enough time to improve your position or mental state before the match starts.

SUCCESS SUMMARY OF PREPARING FOR COMPETITION

By reading and studying the information in this step, you'll have a good idea about what it's going to take to be ready for a match. You should understand how to find matches in your area and what information is included on the match program to help you get ready to participate. After you sign up, set up your prematch routine to account for all the variables that can affect shooting, such as getting enough sleep, eating enough and at the proper time, and getting to the range with enough time to sign in and set up.

After you arrive at the range, continue to follow your routine by setting up your gear and finding time to stretch and relax so that your body is physically ready for the match. Follow a mental routine that helps you focus and accounts for all the mental variables that can affect your performance. Although the 10-minute prep can seem like a long time before you get to shoot, you have a lot to do and make ready before that first shot goes down range.

In the next step we will cover topics from what to expect of the people around you to how matches vary depending on the course of fire and who is hosting the match. Time limits and target height issues will be discussed. You'll learn about how targets are scored and what your options are if you don't agree with the score. You want to get all the points you deserve, and the next step will show you how to get them.

Before Taking the Next Step

Before moving on to step 8, Competing in Matches, evaluate what you have learned to this point. Answer each of the following questions honestly. If you can answer all seven questions, you are ready to move on to the next step.

1. Where do you look to find matches in your area?
2. What organizations use the National Standard Three-Position Air Rifle rules?
3. Whom do you contact to sign up for a match?
4. Why do you need a match program?
5. What kinds of foods give you enough energy to get through a match? How much time do you need after eating before you shoot?
6. What stretches help you get into more comfortable and controlled positions?
7. What is your plan when you get to the range before a match? What do you need to do to be ready to shoot?

Competing in Matches

A notable thing about shooting sports is that anyone can compete. No matter how much experience you have and what your ability level is, you get to step up to the line and compete with everyone else. Those who are attracted to this sport usually have an inner drive to show that they have mastered mind over body. They love to challenge themselves to perform under pressure and find what brings out the best in them when the chips are down. Shooting is like playing a game of chess.

You evaluate your hold that day and try different tactics to control it. After you accomplish that, you discern the timing that it will take to shoot good shots through the hold. You need concentration, intuition, anticipation, and precision to have a great shooting performance. Shooting is much more of a mental sport than it is a physical sport. You can expect the atmosphere at a match to allow shooters to find their own space in which to get organized, mentally and physically.

TOURNAMENT ATMOSPHERE

Building on the prematch timeframe described in step 7, this step explains what to expect from other competitors and line officers, and the kind of atmosphere that these people create at a competition. Remember, you are in charge of how you react to the competitive environment. Be ready to roll with the punches.

After you arrive at a match and check in, other competitors will be nearby. They too will be looking for space to put down their gear and set up. Some friendly competitors will introduce themselves and chat. Others may go into their own private worlds when they get to the range and not want to talk to anyone. Some shooters

may be anxious or nervous and talk as a way to distract themselves. Teams may be talking and joking together, but usually everyone follows some kind of prematch plan to get ready to compete. The best thing to do is be courteous to those around you. If they have headphones on and are quietly stretching, they probably don't want to be disturbed. If they are talking to other people, it's probably fine to introduce yourself.

If you have any questions or concerns, don't hesitate to find a match official or line officer to help you. Although they may yell on the range so that everyone can hear them (and seem

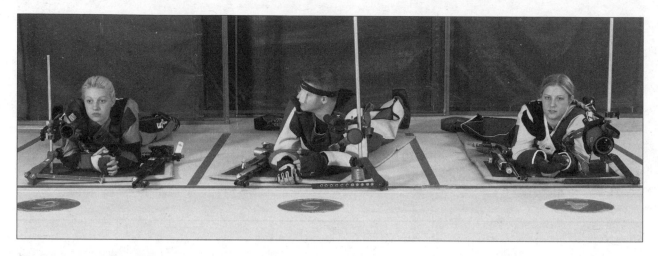

Shooters on the line relaxing before the prep period.

extremely strict on the line), they are also there to help you get to the right location at the right time and answer any questions that you have about the match. Usually they are eager to help. After all, they love the sport enough to spend all day watching others shoot.

The competitive atmosphere is going to be a combination of all these things—competitors checking in and setting up, gear bags everywhere (if it's a small range), some people talking too much and others not at all, line officers calling shooters to the line, and spectators gathered around to offer support.

Review the timeline in step 7 and establish how you want to set up for the match. Choose a method that is efficient and beneficial for you. If talking helps you settle down, find others who like to be social before the match. Don't disturb shooters who want to be quiet. If you can't find other shooters to talk to, talk with your supporters or coach. If you are the organized type, set up your gear so that you don't have to worry if something is out of place. Although you have little control over the atmosphere around you, you are in charge of your internal atmosphere and need to complete all the necessary tasks so that you can perform your best. Have your checklist ready and follow it so that you know you've taken care of everything and are ready to go to work on the range.

NUMBER OF COMPETITORS AND RELAYS

The number of competitors is decided by the match organizers and often depends on the size of the range and the time limit for the match.

If you are shooting at a large range, such as the Olympic Training Center (OTC), Ft. Benning, or Camp Perry, you can expect many other shooters. As many as 100 shooters may be shooting at the same time if the range has 100 points. Competitors may be shooting on different ranges at the same location, and shooters will be moving their equipment between matches. You must keep your gear organized and accounted for so that you are ready to go.

At smaller ranges, match officials will set up relays to get all competitors through the match.

A relay is a group of shooters who shoot on the range at the same time. If a match has 50 competitors and the range has only 10 points to shoot on, five relays of 10 shooters each will be required. The larger the range, the fewer the number of relays will be needed to get all competitors through. In a match like this, you may not even see all the competitors. If you are on the first relay, you likely won't still be around by the time the fifth relay takes the line. Some matches run over a couple of days or a couple of weekends to accommodate a large number of competitors. Some clubs may host tournaments that run every weekend for a month. In matches like these, you'll see only the competitors on your relay, but you'll get a match bulletin that lists how everyone shot after the event is over.

After you send in your entry form, check to see what relay you're shooting on and what time it starts. You'll have a long day if you show up at 7:00 a.m. and don't shoot until 2:00 p.m. Plan your prematch routine accordingly.

For some matches, you may shoot the same course of fire two or three times, usually over

two or more days, for an aggregate score. At other matches, such as NCAA matches, you'll shoot two different matches with two different rifles for a team aggregate score. At matches like these, you may shoot two relays back to back or have to wait while a relay or two shoots between the times when you shoot. When you sign up, you'll be able to see the match courses of fire and plan your routine according to the number of times that you'll shoot that day.

POSITION TARGET HEIGHTS, SHOTS PER POSITION, AND TIME RESTRICTIONS

In matches sponsored by the National Three-Position Air Rifle Council, target heights and times are set by position. Because a time limit is imposed for each position, you will wait until everyone has finished the position being shot before changing your rifle to the next position and continuing the match. Specific target heights

are indicated for each position. The heights listed in tables 8.1 and 8.2 correspond to the center of the target for single-bull targets or the center of the two sighting bulls on 10-bull targets (figure 8.1). The match structure looks like the structure shown in tables 8.1 and 8.2, depending on the course of fire.

Table 8.1 Individual 3 × 10 Event in National Three-Position Air Rifle Council Matches

Position	Target height	Time limit
Prep time	NA	10 min.
10 shots prone position	0.5 m (±10 cm) or 19.7 in. (±4 in.)	20 min.
Changeover period	NA	5 min.
10 shots standing position	1.4 m (±5 cm) or 55 in. (±2 in.)	20 min.
Changeover period	NA	5 min.
10 shots kneeling position	0.8 m (±10 cm) or 31.5 in. (±4 in.)	15 min.

Table 8.2 Individual 3 × 20 Event in National Three-Position Air Rifle Council Matches

Position	Target height	Time limit
Prep time	NA	10 min.
20 shots prone position	0.5 m (± 10 cm) or 19.7 in. (±4 in.)	30 min.
Changeover period	NA	5 min.
20 shots standing position	1.4 m (±5 cm) or 55 in. (±2 in.)	40 min.
Changeover period	NA	5 min.
20 shots kneeling position	0.8 m (±10 cm) or 31.5 in. (±4 in.)	30 min.

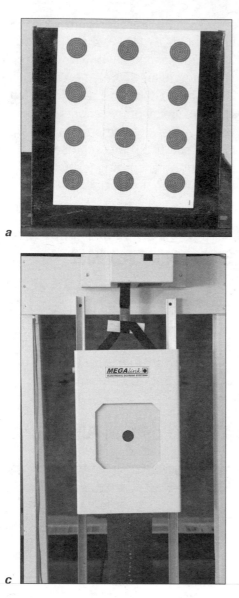

Figure 8.1 Target setups: (*a*) paper 10 bull; (*b*) electronic single bull monitor; and *(c)* target system.

You will notice a discrepancy in the time limits for the positions in table 8.1. Extra time is given in the prone position to allow for sighting in. Ten or 15 minutes is a short amount of time to get a rifle sighted in and shoot 10 quality shots down range. Competitions that follow national standard rules are the only matches that provide extra time for sighting in during prone position. Usually you have only 1 or 1 1/2 minutes per shot, including sighting shots, in prone position. You'll get 2 minutes per shot in standing position, and 1 1/2 minutes per shot in kneeling position.

Other situations at a match can influence time and targets. For example, some targets may be fixed at one height (usually the international standing height of 1.4 m). If this is the case, the range will provide tables for you to shoot on in prone and kneeling positions. The tables allow you to raise your body to the correct height so that you can shoot at the fixed-height target.

Some electronic targets come with movable lifts that move the targets up and down. But on some ranges the targets may be fixed for a different set height in prone, standing, and kneeling positions.

Outdoor ranges (common in Hawaii and warmer climates) include wind flags to show the strength and direction of the wind. You must learn to shoot with different wind, lighting, and weather if you plan to shoot on outdoor ranges.

The NRA uses slightly different rules. As a rule of thumb, the NRA allows 1 1/2 minutes per shot for prone and kneeling positions and 2 minutes per shot for standing position. The NRA also recommends that the standing target height be 1.4 meters (the same as the other types of matches) and that the other position heights be adjustable within the range of the target holders. This rule means that you can shoot your targets at whatever height you choose, as long as the target holders can be adjusted to that height. Tables 8.3 and 8.4 show typical match formats for NRA competitions.

A shorter time is given for prone position in an NRA 3 × 10 match. You have 15 minutes to get your rifle sighted in and complete your 10 shots. If you don't get all your shots off, you will have 10 points deducted for each unfired shot, which is called a miss. Also notice that you may have a longer changeover period at an NRA match. Be sure to check the match program to see how much time you'll have between positions. If you get only 5 minutes but you are used to 10 or 15, you'll be caught short when the line officer starts the time for the next position.

International matches may have a standing-only match that consists of 60 standing shots for men and 40 standing shots for women. The NCAA college rifle air gun match is also 60 shots from standing position. Check to see whether any of these types of matches are being shot in your area to help you prepare for Junior Olympic and college competition. Standing-only matches use the two-minute-per-shot timing rule with target changeovers after each 20 shots, or they may use block time.

Table 8.3 Individual 3 × 10 Event in National Rifle Association Matches

Position	Time limit
Prep time	10 min.
10 shots prone position	15 min.
Changeover period	5 to 15 min.
10 shots standing position	20 min.
Changeover period	5 to 15 min.
10 shots kneeling position	15 min.

Table 8.4 Individual 3 × 20 Event in National Rifle Association Matches

Position	Time limit
Prep time	10 min.
20 shots prone position	30 min.
Changeover period	5 to 15 min.
20 shots standing position	40 min.
Changeover period	5 to 15 min.
20 shots kneeling position	30 min.

Block time is a total amount of time given to shoot the whole match, including all sighting, record shots, and changeovers. Most international air rifle and small-bore matches held at ranges with electronic or retrievable targets are set up this way. Retrievable targets allow a shooter to bring the target back to her or his point, change targets, and send the target down range again without stepping over the firing line. Some ranges have automatic target carriers. The shooter presses or holds down a button to bring the targets forward or take it back. Some ranges use manual targets (figure 8.2). The shooter cranks the target to and from the firing line.

Depending on how much time is allowed for changeovers within the block time for the match, a 3 × 20 match usually runs for two hours. Some matches may give more time if it takes longer to retrieve and change targets. That decision is up to the match director and will be printed in the program.

Figure 8.2 Range with a crank target system.

MATCH START

By this point, you have finished your prep period, checked your natural point of aim, and are relaxed so that you are ready to go. The line officer announces, "Your preparation period has ended. Is the line ready?" If you are not ready for some reason—your target has fallen, something broke on your rifle, or you see someone doing an unsafe act—raise your hand and say, "Not ready on target 4," or whatever your target number is. This call will alert the range officer that something needs to be corrected before the match can begin. The range officer will say, "The line is not ready." After the problem has been corrected, the range officer will say, "The line is ready. Commence fire" (or "Start"). The line officer may conclude by saying, "You have 30 minutes," or whatever time is given for that position or match. When this command is given, load your rifle and begin shooting.

SIGHTING IN

Now that the relay on the line is starting to shoot, load your rifle and assume your natural position at your first sighting bull (figure 8.3). Sighting bulls are easy to identify because they have a large black triangle at the corner or a ring around them in the center of the target.

Shoot as many shots as you want to at your sighting bulls. Just remember that after you go for record, which means that you are shooting one shot per record bull to be scored, you are not allowed to go back to your sighting bulls. You must have a plan of action for sighting in the rifle that will prepare you and increase your confidence when the time comes to go for record.

Figure 8.3 Sighting bull.

Here's what you want to accomplish in your sighting shots:

• **Make sure that the rifle is working properly.** Check that your sights are on tight, that your cylinder is full of air, and that nothing on your rifle is out of place. Although you checked all these items during setup and the prep period, after you are actually shooting shots through the barrel you may find that something is out of place or broken, such as a trigger.

• **Get your hold under control and as small as possible.** Although you worked on this during the prep period by dry firing, when you are shooting shots through that hold, the focus becomes more intense. Evaluate what your hold looks like on that day and adjust to control it, concentrating to make it as small as possible.

• **Adjust your sights to the center of the target.** After your hold is under control, start taking shots with the intent to get sighted in. Shoot three to five shots to see where the rifle is grouping. The word *grouping* describes a group of shots. Try to shoot a group before moving your sights. If you move your sights after every shot, you'll end up chasing yourself around the target and never get sighted in. Some shooters shoot three shots before they even look in the scope. This helps them focus on taking quality shots instead of where the shots are hitting the target. After you think that you have a group, click your sights to move the center of the group to the center of the target. A critical detail to know before shooting a match is how many clicks per ring it takes to move your sights. Most sights move 4 to 6 clicks per ring, depending on the quality of the sight. Some higher-level sights move 10 clicks per ring, but international prone shooters are usually the only shooters who use these highly sophisticated sights.

An example of sighting in is shown in figure 8.4. The first target shows a shooter's first group. The second target shows the second group, which was shot after the shooter clicked the sights. Notice that the group size is pretty consistent but that it has now moved over the center of the target. This shooter knew exactly how many clicks it took to move the group up and over to the center. If you don't know how many clicks it takes to move a group over a specific distance, you'll waste a lot of time in the sighting bulls, trying to get your shots into the 10 ring. Instead of moving on to focus on timing and other factors, you will be making a trail leading to the 10 ring and still trying to get centered.

- **Refine your timing to take shots going into the 10 ring.** After you are sighted in and are confident that shots are going where you call them, you are ready to buckle down and refine your timing. During a match, you will be a bit excited and may have butterflies because you really want to perform to your full potential. This eagerness can affect your hold and timing. Through practice, develop a solid shot plan to help you perform under the excitement of competition. Because your hold may move a little faster and the time that you settle on the 10 ring may be shorter, sharpen your attention to identify when your hold is going into the 10 ring and settling. When your attention sharpens, so will your reaction time. In this phase of sighting in, work on shooting shots going into the 10 ring and being proactive in controlling them. You may shoot more sighting shots in this phase of the action plan than any other.

- **Get mentally ready to go for record.** You will enter the final phase of sighting in after you are confident that the rifle is shooting where you are calling shots and that you are taking shots at the proper time through your hold. Your follow-through should also be staying on target, and the rifle should feel as if it's a part of you. The final phase is to take two or three more shots just as you would when going for record. This approach helps initiate rhythm, lets you analyze that rhythm, and provides that final vote of confidence that you are ready to perform. After you establish that rhythm and you're rolling with it, you're ready to go for record.

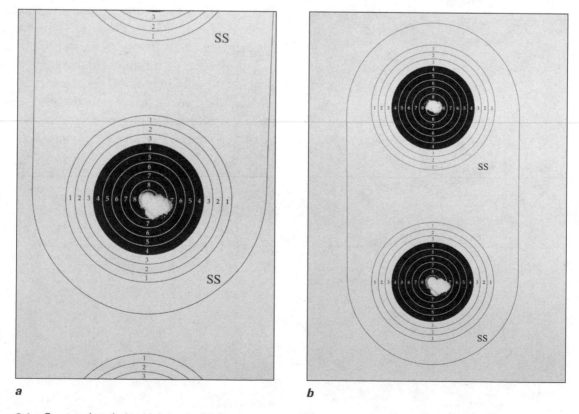

a   b

Figure 8.4 Groups shot during sighting in (a) first group; (b) second group, shot after shooter clicked the sights.

GOING FOR RECORD

Taking that first shot for record can be dramatic and challenging to many shooters. If you follow the action plan for sighting in discussed in the previous section, that first shot will feel less dramatic and more controlled, like an extension of the timing and rhythm pattern that you established during sighting in. The first shot for record is the time to show what kind of shooter you are. You trained and worked hard in practice. Stepping to the line and looking inside yourself to perform to your full potential is the reason that you are in the sport. Shooting for record can and should be the part that you enjoy the most. Although competition can be uncomfortable and challenging, after all the dust has settled, this is the part that you need to live for in your shooting.

With that momentum as fuel, let's look at shooting the first few shots. Because you've been shooting sighters at a sighting bull, you'll need to adjust your position to the first record bull (when shooting a 10-bull target). Many shooters become so locked on to their sighting bulls that they forget to change their natural point of aim (NPA) to the first record bull. I've had to score many 9s that were shot in the direction of the sighting bull because the shooters didn't change their NPA. If those shooters had double-checked their NPA and relaxed, they would have seen that they either didn't move at all or didn't move enough to get their hold to the center of the first record bull. Part of your going-for-record plan needs to include double checking your NPA on the first record bull.

If you are shooting on single-bull targets and changing the target after each shot or shooting electronic targets, your target location will remain the same for your sighters and for record shots. Do not take it for granted that your NPA and position will be the same for the whole match. Over the period of a match, your position can settle or relax as you become more comfortable shooting, or tension may creep in if your endurance is low and your body has to start working harder to maintain position. These body changes can affect your NPA, so continue to check it often throughout a match even though the target stays in the same place and your feet haven't moved.

Many shooters give extra effort to make the first shot successful. They stare and stare at the sight picture to make extra sure that they shoot it when it is exactly centered. They let two or three good shots go by while waiting for something better and end up overholding and shooting a shot that is past the point of being successful. Usually they want to wait to be sure that the shot will stay in the 10 ring. Remember that your hold and timing will be different from day to day. You need to rely on what you learned from your sighters. Try to repeat what worked when you shot your last sighting shots. If they were solid shots, continue with the blueprint that you used to shoot them. You may put the gun down a couple of times, but doing that is much better than overholding and taking a shot that is overworked with an eye that is overstrained.

ADJUSTMENTS DURING COMPETITION

With practice and experience, you will be able to get into your match rhythm quickly and begin to trust your hold and timing. Even if you sight in perfectly, get your first few shots right where you called them, and feel in control of the match and your body, things may shift or settle throughout the match that will require you to reassess and regroup.

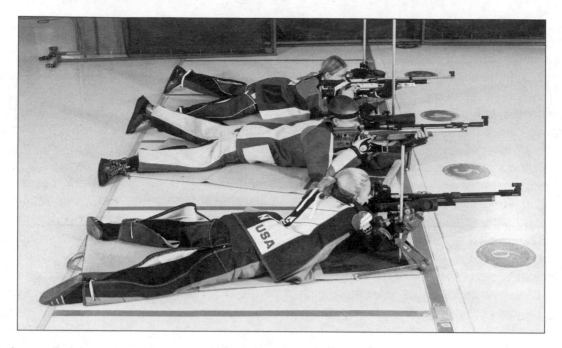

During the match, focus on your position and target.

Click Sights

Don't be afraid to adjust your sights after you've gone for record. Many shooters think that after they've sighted in and have some successful on-call shots, their rifles are set for the whole match. Your body will settle or relax during a match, and you may end up placing your cheek on your cheek piece slightly differently because of relaxation in your shoulders and neck. You may need 15 minutes before you relax to the point at which you have the best cheek piece placement for your head and neck. Changes in cheek placement will cause you to look through your sights slightly differently. A slight change won't cause you to shoot wild shots, but it may be enough to cause you to shoot 10s consistently to the left or right instead of in the middle of the target. If you shoot two or three shots in the same direction when you thought that they should have been centered, don't hesitate to move your sights one or two clicks to get those shots back over the 10. Don't settle for just nudging the 10 ring; knock it out!

Before you click, though, make sure that you are looking through your sights correctly. Check that the rear and front sights are perfectly aligned and that your front aperture is centered on the target before you add clicks. During a

match you can be so caught up in centering the front aperture that you forget to check the rear and front sight alignment first. Neglecting sight alignment will cause off-call shots. The problem isn't that your position has settled; it's that you are not attending to the whole sight picture.

Refocus

Advanced shooters have a specific shot plan, focus, and rhythm to their performance. Developing and perfecting shot plans and competition plans requires a lot of practice and experience. These plans include refocusing. Advanced shooters know that almost anything can happen in competition. You should try to avoid being rattled or shaken by things that are outside your control or even within it.

Targets may fall or malfunction, pellets can jam, sights can come loose, other shooters may become upset or act out, a range officer may tell you that something with your equipment is illegal, you may shoot a couple of bad shots in a row, you may shoot better than you ever have, or you may find yourself shooting next to the best shooter in the country. Many things can happen in a match. The point is to be prepared when something does happen. If it takes you away from your focus and competition plan, have a plan of action to get you back in the game.

If something happens to your rifle or target and you can't shoot, raise your hand to bring the line officer over to you. Let him or her know that you have a malfunction and ask the line officer to note the time. If you have a target or rifle malfunction, you will have time to fix it (usually up to 15 minutes) and then be given extra time to finish your match, including taking unlimited sighters before you return to record shots. If the problem takes longer than 15 minutes to correct, the chief range officer will decide how to proceed. You may need to finish the match on another point or with another rifle. Even when something critical happens, keep calm. You will have enough time to finish the match without being rushed to do so.

After something like this happens, take a moment to refocus when you are back on the line and able to shoot again. If you are flustered or upset, set down the rifle, take some deep breaths, and think about getting inside yourself and calming down. Remember, what's going on in your head usually ends up on your target. If your mind is full of negative, frustrated images and words, more likely than not your shots will follow suit. Taking the time that you need to get in control of your thoughts and body will serve you well as you continue the match. Follow this sequence to get back under control and refocus for the match:

1. Close your eyes and take some deep breaths.

2. Breathe with your abdomen, not your chest.

3. Think of a calm, comfortable place.

4. Let your body relax. Feel the tension drain away.

5. When your breathing, body, and mind are relaxed, image a perfect sight picture.

6. Fill your mind with the image that you want to create with your sights and target.

7. Breathe while thinking about shooting a shot through the image and getting a perfect 10.

8. Open your eyes, check your body for tension, check your NPA, and dry-fire a few times.

You should now be back in the present, feeling ready to shoot again. Don't let the past influence the present. Even if something negative has happened, stop dwelling on it or worrying about it. If you worry, the problem has control of what you're trying to accomplish in the present. Don't give it any weight or let it pull on you. Learn from it, let it go, and be strong to focus on what it takes to shoot one successful shot at a time.

SCORING

Scoring is usually done in a location separate from the shooters and range. Shooters are not allowed in the scoring area, and the targets are all brought out after the scoring so that the shooters can check them during the challenge period. Paper targets are scored by a team. Two people look at each shot. If they agree on the value they move on to the next shot. If the shot looks too close to call, the scorers use a scoring gauge or plug. They place a plug in the shot hole and use the outside edge of the plug to determine whether a shot is in or out. If the outside edge of the plug is tangent or inside the next scoring ring, it is called "in." The scorers mark that the shot was plugged and give it a

+ sign, which means the higher value (figure 8.5a). If the outside edge of the plug crosses the next scoring ring, it is called "out." The scorers mark a − sign next to it, indicating the lower value (figure 8.5b).

After a shot is plugged and evaluated by two people (a third is used if the first two scorers can't agree on the value), it can't be plugged again. A shot is plugged only once, and the shot value is final. No protest can be made against it.

If a shot hasn't been plugged and you don't agree with the value that it was given, you can challenge the score (usually you have to pay a small fee) and have the judges or other scorers

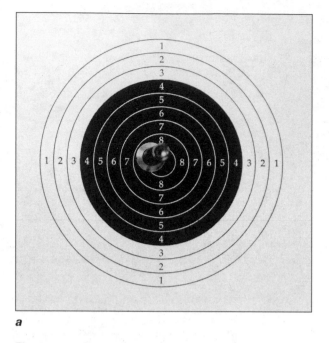

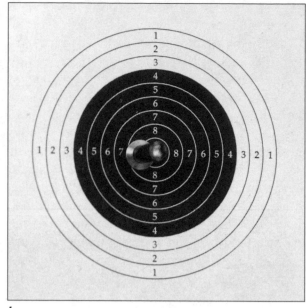

a

b

Figure 8.5 Plugged shots: (*a*) shot is in; (*b*) shot is out.

plug it. If you win the challenge, you get your fee back. You can challenge your score for only a certain amount of time after a match, during an interval called the challenge period, which usually lasts 30 to 60 minutes after the targets are brought out from the scorers' tables.

After all the shots are scored, a total is given for all 10 shots on that target (figure 8.6). The total that you will see is your score out of 100 points. All your targets will be listed on the results board as well as how you compare to the rest of the relay.

You should always check your targets. Sometimes shots are scored incorrectly, and sometimes totals are added incorrectly. You are responsible for double checking that the score you received is accurate. If the scorers gave you more points than you deserved, bring that to their attention as well. Get the score that you shot, not the one that the scorers may have inaccurately given you. You would want other shooters to do the same.

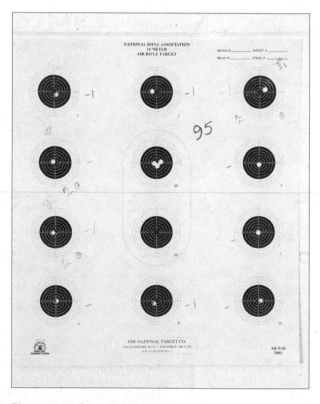

Figure 8.6 Scored target.

SUCCESS SUMMARY OF COMPETING IN TOURNAMENTS

You have moved into becoming a competitive shooter through the experiences described in this step. From creating a mental and physical strategy to prepare yourself for competition to following a plan to make your first shot for record smooth as silk, you are starting to discover what makes you tick as a competitive shooter and how you can adjust the elements of your plan to fit your needs.

By this point, you should have a clear understanding of the time limits involved in the matches that you shoot and the preparation required for the various types of targets and carriers that you may be using at those locations. Each range will feature something unique. Look at that as an advantage. Viewing it that way helps you become a well-rounded shooter who can roll with the punches no matter what challenge or change arises. You will always be provided your own space, on your own point, with your own rifle. Use your strategy to show what kind of shooter you are, no matter what the circumstances. You want to make the most of your time and space and not let outside obstacles control you.

Now that you have a good understanding of the strategy involved in setting up for a match, getting sighted in, getting ready to go for record, and shooting the entire match, learn to put those elements to work in training so that you are efficient and prepared to meet the challenges of competition. In the next step, you'll start by building a shooter's journal to track your progress in training and competition. You'll learn drills to help you with various aspects of the match and the season. You'll do competitive drills with teammates and individual drills to push your concentration and endurance limits. Let's move on and get into some great shooting.

Before Taking the Next Step

Before moving to step 9, Practicing for Optimal Performance, evaluate what you have learned to this point. Answer each of the following questions honestly. If you are able to answer all six questions, you are ready to move on to the next step.

1. Do you know the time structure of the match that you're going to shoot?

2. What is block time?

3. Do you have a strategy for sighting in the rifle, or do you go for record after shooting your first 10 in the sighting bull?

4. Should you move your sights during a match after you have sighted in and gone for record?

5. If some circumstance challenges you during a match, what is a good refocus routine to follow to get you back into your match mind-set?

6. How do you know whether a shot has been plugged?

Practicing for Optimal Performance

Having been a shooter since 1978 and in coaching since 1994, I know that as much as I'd like to believe in natural talent and overnight sensations, no magic charms or quick fixes can instantly make someone a great shooter. Shooting is a sport that takes some natural talent, but it requires sustained work over time to turn talent into true ability. Although natural talent helps in the beginning, it makes up about 1 percent of a top-level shooter's ability. Hard work and dedication make up the rest.

Even if you have natural talent, you will need practice and experience to hone that talent into the kind of ability required to succeed at higher levels. Many shooters who are told that they have natural talent think that they can bypass training and let their natural ability carry them. It carries them only a short way past where they start. Dedication and determination are the elements needed to turn talent into ability. Don't depend on natural talent to carry you through your shooting career. If you do, you will have a short one.

For those who want to take their talent to its full potential and become the best shooters that they can be, the practice and training options in this step can help.

SHOOTER'S JOURNAL

The most important tool in a shooter's toolbox is a journal. You can use this instrument to track rifle settings, your progress, ways to overcome challenges or obstacles, wisdom gained through experience, goals, and personal records. Take it to practice and matches so that you can record discoveries or areas that you need to work on. With many settings per position to track, with a multitude of elements in a shot plan and competition plan to develop, you can easily miss an item or take for granted things that you need to account for. You can save time and frustration by keeping your journal nearby to remind you of the many important items that go into a task. Because everyone has limited time to practice and focus on his or her shooting, you benefit by not having to relearn a lesson or overcome the same challenge that you faced a month ago. Tracking those challenges and their solutions in your journal will help in the long run. You will not have to repeat unsuccessful attempts and may even be able to avoid obstacles completely.

Here are some suggestions for the type of information to keep in your journal.

Personal Information

Write your name, address, phone numbers, and e-mail address in your journal. If you accidentally leave it somewhere, the person who finds it will be able to contact you. Enter your coach's contact information as well.

Include contact information for the NRA, USA Shooting, and National Standard Three-Position Air Rifle Council. Be sure to add your membership numbers for these organizations (NRA, USA Shooting, etc.) and others that you belong to. You will need those numbers when you sign up for a match or fill out paperwork.

Write down your rifle model and serial number, in case you need the information when you are traveling, buying new items for your rifle, or having your rifle worked on. In addition, include the pellet brand and size that you prefer.

Rifle, Clothing, and Position Settings

For prone position, note rifle settings, clothing information, and position comments:

- Rifle for prone: butt plate height and distance; cheek piece, hand stop, and sight locations; front aperture and rear iris settings.

- Clothing for prone: jacket buttons to use, shoulder adjustment strap, sling adjustment and angle on arm, visor, mat angle, target height (if adjustable).

- Position for prone: comments from your training and the observations of your coach.

Have photos taken of your prone position from different angles and insert them into your journal. Identify the angle that you use toward the target and have your mat placed up to the firing line and at that angle. Mark where you want to place your pivot elbow on the mat (as close to the firing line as possible). Mark where you should place your other elbow. Remember

that this elbow will move as your natural point of aim moves. This starting point supports your best position.

Have a photo taken from the side that shows your head and your eyes looking through your sights. Identify the distance from your eye to the sight. Note that your head is level. Have another photo taken of your finger on the trigger to show the angle of your wrist. This view can include your hand stop and support hand under the fore-end stock. Identify the angle of the arm supporting the stock. You can go back to this reference if you think that something isn't right with your position. Have someone look at the position that you are in and compare it to the photo in your journal.

For standing position, you want to note comments in the same categories—rifle, clothing, and position:

- Rifle for standing: butt plate height and distance, cheek piece and sight locations, front aperture and rear iris settings.

- Clothing for standing: belt, shoulder adjustment strap, visor, target height (if adjustable).

- Position for standing: comments from your training and the observations of your coach.

Obtain photos of your standing position from all four angles. Identify the starting placement for your feet and the distance between them from the side-angle photo. Remember that foot placement will change as your natural point of aim changes up and down or if your target is at a different height than what you are accustomed to. Identify the angles of your feet. Identify the height of the rifle as it goes across your body and the location of the butt plate on your arm or armpit. Mark the angle of the arm that is supporting the rifle and where that hand is under the stock. Mark the distance of your eye from the sight and note whether your head tilts forward. From a photo taken from the rear, identify the cant of the rifle and the way that your head meets the cheek piece. Also, look at the shape of your back and the amount of arch. A photo from the front will show whether the gun is resting on the front side of the jacket, which is illegal. That view can also show head, neck, and back angles. Remember to take photos after you develop a position that allows you to shoot successfully. If you make changes, practice them awhile and then take new photos. Keep all of your photos, maybe in another notebook, to show the progression and evolution of your positions, noting when they improved and why.

For kneeling position, you want to note comments in the same categories—rifle, clothing, and position:

- Rifle for kneeling: butt-plate height and distance; cheek piece, hand stop, and sight locations; front aperture and rear iris settings.

- Clothing for kneeling: jacket buttons to use, pants open, shoulder adjustment strap, sling adjustment and angle on arm, visor, kneeling roll angle, way boots are tied to accommodate the shape of the kneeling roll, target height (if adjustable).

- Position for kneeling: comments from your training and the observations of your coach.

Have photos taken of you in kneeling position from all angles. Identify the body position that works best. Obtain a photo from the front of the position to see that the rifle is just to the right of and above the left knee, that the right shoulder is mostly facing forward, and that the left leg is perpendicular to the floor, not angled right or left. A photo from the right side will show the butt plate fitted into your shoulder; the angle of your right wrist, the distance from your eye to the sight; the cheek piece, head, and hand-stop positions; and the angle of your left arm supporting the rifle. A photo from the rear will show the straight line from the toe of the boot on the kneeling roll to the top of your head. The photo should show that the boot is square on the kneeling roll, that the foot is straight up and down, and that the heel meets the tailbone. A picture from the left will show left-arm place-

ment and, if the left foot is out, the left foot set more toward the target.

In addition, have close-up photos taken of your rifle after it is set up in each position. Add a written description next to the photo, noting where your settings are for each item. Mark the settings on the pictures as well. That way you can easily identify and repeat the correct settings. Many shooters mark lines on their rifles to indicate where the butt plate, cheek piece, hand stop, and sights should go. That method is fine, but try not to erase the marks as you move adjustable items over them. Be sure to erase old lines as you change the locations of those items. You don't want to have to decipher five lines on the butt plate during a match.

Goals

Goal setting will be covered in more detail in the next step. Have a section of your journal dedicated to your goals and dreams. These items fuel your motivation and excitement to be involved in the sport. Knowing that you are on track to accomplish a challenge that you set before yourself is a great feeling. Reviewing your goals and dreams can help you reflect on the larger picture when the going gets tough. Include long-term goals, short-term goals, and intrinsic and extrinsic goals. Write how you will use each of these goals in your training plan.

Training Plans

This section will hold your annual and season training plans. For each month of the season, note the matches that you will shoot, the days that you have for training, and the emphasis that you will place on each part of the season. Before the season starts, be sure your rifle and gear are working properly. A gunsmith may need a while to fix a broken rifle, and you don't want to waste time during the season taking care of this task.

You should dedicate the first part of the season, the prematch phase, to establishing positions, setting your rifle and gear to your body, and shooting consistently. Your focus in training should be on quantity so that you can build shot plans and improve timing, endurance, concentration, and position repeatability. Depending on how much time you have before matches start, this period can include a couple of weeks to a couple of months of training time.

The second part of the season, the match phase, is focused on preparing for matches, building competition plans, refocusing plans, and gaining control of positions and thinking. The training focus shifts to quality, but do not give up on quantity just yet. You will start shooting league or school matches, and practice will focus on preparing for that level of competition. This phase can last for months, depending on the kind and number of matches that you have in your area.

The third part of the season, the championship phase, is dedicated to perfecting your skills and getting ready for the biggest competition of the season. Focus on getting the job done with the number of shots available in the match, not on large quantities of shots. In three-position air rifle, you have 20 shots in each position. Training needs to reflect this demand so that you can build the right plan for the job. This phase of the season focuses on quality. Raise your level of effort to match the conditions of the season-ending match that you are preparing for. This phase of the season may be only a month long, depending on the matches that you shoot. If you don't have a championship to prepare for, pick the last match of the season to focus on as your championship match to provide a culmination point.

Each of these phases will be covered in more detail later in this step. Include in your journal a calendar with enough space for each month to describe what phase of the season you are working on.

Practice Plans and Evaluation

You'll use this section daily. Write down what you want to accomplish and work on before you get to the range. Many people do this after evaluating their last practice so that they stay on track. Know what areas and positions you want to work on so that you don't waste your limited training time. When you show up at the range with a clear daily training plan in mind, you will be more productive and more likely to accomplish your daily goals, taking you a step closer to your match goals. Figure 9.1 shows a sample two-week practice plan.

Some shooters develop a one- or two-week focus plan. This approach helps them prepare and stay on track for longer stretches of time. After the second week, they reassess to see whether they are on track to meet their monthly or short-term goals. This will be discussed in more depth in step 11.

For your practice plans, identify two or three tasks to work on during practice that day. These tasks should lead you to a specific accomplishment for the week (or two-week period). Try to work at least two positions per practice session to help you learn to transition between positions during a match. This approach also gives your body a break so that you are not overextending yourself in any one position by training for hours at a time. By just identifying specific tasks to focus on, you'll accomplish more.

Track the number of shots that you put down range as well. This record can help when analyzing goals. If you have weeks when you achieve little or no improvement, increase the number of shots during practice to see whether that helps. To change the number of shots, you need to know how many you are shooting. Analyze as well the number of days that you're able to train. If three days a week isn't enough, you may need to train at home on days that you can't get to the range. Dry-fire or perform holding exercises every day, if you can.

Track what tasks you focus on and how they improve your performance. Track the evolution of your shot plan as well as your training intensity as it increases and the plan becomes more automatic. Identifying these factors and working on them will improve performance.

When something is working, write it down so that you can remember it and repeat it later. List all the factors that went into a good performance and put them into your shot and competition plans. Be responsible for them. When the chips are down, these are the factors that you can rely on because you've proven it in practice.

Sample Two-Week Practice Plan

Practice Plan for Sept. 1-14   Current ability level: _____

What I'd like to shoot in two weeks of training: _____

My focus for this training period: _____
(for example, quantity and position training)

Performance goals for this training period

1. _____

2. _____

3. _____

Plan of Action

Monday: 100 shots standing, 50 shots kneeling, focus is on building positions and endurance.

Results of training: (write what you learned from the day) _____

Tuesday: 100 shots kneeling, 50 shots prone, focus is on repeating position and endurance.

Results of training: _____

Wednesday: Off

Thursday: 100 shots prone, 60 standing, focus is on when to take breaks to keep shooting 10s.

Results of training: _____

Friday: 40 shots prone, 40 shots standing, 40 shots kneeling, focus is on building endurance and getting efficient at changing over to other positions.

Saturday and Sunday: Dry firing at home in standing for 30 minutes each day.

Monday: 80 shots standing, 60 shots kneeling, focus is on timing and endurance.

Results of training: _____

Tuesday: 80 shots kneeling, 80 shots prone, focus is on timing and endurance.

Results of training: _____

Wednesday: Dry firing at home in standing for 30 minutes.

Thursday: 40 shots prone, 40 standing, and 40 kneeling. Focus is on endurance and position changeover.

Results of training: _____

Friday: Practice the two positions that were the most challenging from Thursday. Get into the positions, get sighted in, think about going for record, and then train 30 shots in each.

Results of training: _____

Saturday: Practice match, 20 shots prone, 20 shots standing, and 20 kneeling. Coach scores the targets. Prone score: _____ Standing score: _____ Kneeling score: _____

Results from practice match: (write what you learned and what you will work on for the next two weeks of training) _____

(continued)

Figure 9.1 Week from a sample practice plan.

(continued)

Goals achieved

1. _____

2. _____

3. _____

Goals to work on:

(do you just need more time to achieve the goals set two weeks ago, or do you need to change your training strategy, like shooting more shots, doing more dry firing, or performing more practice matches?)

1. _____

2. _____

3. _____

Figure 9.1   *(continued)*

At the back of the practice evaluations section, add a match wisdom section. (See the sample in figure 9.2.) On this page, list specific items that you can rely on or that you need to remember during a match. Instead of thumbing through all your practice sections to solve a problem, simply flip open to this page. Reserve this section for recurring issues that you address on a regular basis. It may contain position-specific wisdom or mental tactics that you use in a certain situation. This is the refined wisdom that you've learned throughout your training and match experience. It should be specific and positive and provide known solutions.

Match Experience

In this section, track all your matches. Learn from each competitive experience in a constructive and positive way. Include the following items in your match experience section. Some of these items are important on the day of the match, but you will use most of this information to prepare for upcoming competitions.

Include the match date, location, and name. Add directions for getting to the match if it is in an unfamiliar location. When you get to the range, note the range conditions:

- Number of firing points
- Lighting conditions (do you need a visor because of overhead lighting conditions?)
- Amount of room per point
- Amount of space for gear
- Location of the range clock (is it easy to see, or do you need your timer?)
- Kind of targets and target carriers

Take a photo of the range for future reference and put it in your journal.

Set goals for the match, which may include a scoring range. Be sure to include task goals that will help you achieve your scoring goal.

Note your physical condition before, during, and after the match:

- Are you hydrated?
- When did you eat? Do you feel full or hungry?
- Do your muscles feel relaxed and ready? Do you need to stretch?
- Do you feel any tension? If so, identify it and relieve it.

Match Wisdom Page Example

For prone:

- Keep checking right-elbow placement.
- Double-check cheek placement.
- Relax shoulders.

For standing:

- Relax legs.
- Keep right arm strong but elbow down.
- Cant the rifle in.
- Let the rifle settle twice. Tf the shot doesn't go off, put the gun down!

For kneeling:

- Build position without the rifle. If the position doesn't settle, get out and start over.
- Spend time with eyes closed to see whether position wants to drift.
- Make sure that pants and back of right boot are open!

For shot plan:

- Stay in the present. If past or future issues creep in, deal with them constructively so that you can move on. Don't pick up the gun if you're thinking about the past or the end of the match.
- Do the body check, the position check, and the sight check.
- End with an image of the perfect sight picture.
- Let everything go so you are ready to react to the 10.
- Trust.

Figure 9.2 Sample match wisdom page.

Note your mental condition before, during, and after the match:

- Are you focused?
- Do you believe in your goals and feel confident and challenged about them?
- Are you ready to follow your competition plan?
- What is your level of excitement? Do you need to relax or energize?
- Do you have a positive mental attitude?
- Is your self-talk in check?

Record your match results: prone, standing, and kneeling scores and your final score. After your scores, add a section on evaluation. Here you write about what happened, what things you worked on, how they helped or what you still need to improve, and anything else that you learned that will help your next performance. Many shooters write about negative experiences but it is important keep track of everything that went right as well. Tracking the positive aspects of the performance will help build confidence and excitement for the next competition. Some items to track in this section include consistency in getting the rifle into the correct place, position stability, balance and hold, breath control, consistent sight picture and focus, trigger control, timing, follow-through, and calling the shot.

Sometimes shooters say, "My performance was better than my score." Usually they are reflecting on specific tasks that they worked on during the match but that didn't positively affect their score. For example, although their timing may have been off, their position consistency and follow-through may have been excellent. Shooters who make comments like this still have work to do before the positive aspects of their shooting will show up in their score at match time. They need to adjust their focus during the match.

Celebrate milestones as you accomplish them. The more you write, talk, and think about the goals that you have accomplished and the challenges that you've overcome, the more confident you will be going into the next phase of competition.

Include a score chart (figure 9.3) to track your scores over a season. You can generate a score chart on a computer or keep a simple grid in your journal. Use the chart as a motivational tool or a confidence builder as you see that line of scores continue to rise.

At the end of the match section, include more match wisdom. Write in this section after analyzing the match. Because information stays fresh for only a short time, write down the things that you learned before you forget them. This section isn't the detailed critique that you'll write in the evaluation section. Record here specific

Shooters on the line shooting a final. Be sure to record match results and comments in your shooter's journal.

MATCH SCORES										
600										
595										
590										
585										
580										579
575						570	574			
570				566	567					
565		565				563			564	
560	562		559							
555										
550										
545										
540										
535										
530										
	20-Sep	4-Oct	18-Oct	1-Nov	15-Nov	6-Dec	10-Jan	24-Jan	14-Feb	28-Feb
MATCH DATES										

Figure 9.3 Score chart.

items of important information so that you can find them quickly during a match. For example, you may have used a cue word that helped you focus before a shot. You may have overcome a balance issue by focusing on butt plate placement so that the rifle was in a better spot. You can use these fixes in the future. Don't allow the good solutions to escape.

RANGE PRACTICE

Now that your rifle is set up, your positions are established, and your journal is ready for you to add information, let's go to the range for training. This section covers each phase of the season, providing training techniques to complement the areas that you are working on during that phase. You will learn the physical aspects to focus on, practice drills, shot plan development and refinement, mental training elements to add, and other tips to help you get the most out of your training time.

Prematch Phase

Physical training during the prematch phase focuses on making positions consistent and reliable. Build balance and stability by shooting a lot of rounds, performing holding exercises, and dry firing at home. Your body will build endurance and concentration during this time as you work on specific elements of each shot for longer periods.

Practice Drills

At first, shooting is fun and exciting because it's new, challenging, and rewarding. Your scores seem to go up every time you pick up the gun. But when you get serious about the sport and pick up the gun daily, some of that newness wears off. You may start to feel as if you're doing the same thing day in and day out, which may hamper your desire to make progress. Adding different drills and training methods can cause a change in perspective and focus to help keep training fun and rewarding.

The drills that follow are developed for the prematch phase. They will help you identify the physical elements that go into creating and maintaining a solid position. After the prematch phase ends, you can continue to use some of these drills to help you warm up, or you can revisit a training technique that helped you overcome a position problem.

Prematch Drill 1.   *Getting In and Out of Position*

Improving position reliability includes getting in and out of position a number of times until you can consistently assume the same solid position. If something changes or breaks down when you reassume the position, you'll know that you need to address one element or another.

One thing to look for is rifle balance. Ask yourself whether the rifle feels solid. You should not have the feeling that it wants to fall or drift away from you. Loosen your grip on the pistol grip. If the rifle leans, make adjustments to the rifle or check the angles of your body.

When your position doesn't feel correct or something shifts while you're shooting, you need the confidence to get out of position, check the rifle or other items that might be out of place, and then get back into position and continue shooting. Many shooters are afraid to get out of position, especially after they go for record. They are fearful about upsetting what they do have and don't have the confidence to create a better position. The possibility of shooting poor shots because of a breakdown in position should motivate you to get up and correct something that is within your control. Believe that the problem is within your control. Because attaining this confidence takes training, you must practice getting in and out of position, not only to check that you are consistent each time but also to build the confidence to reestablish your position under match conditions.

After you set up a position, write down all the important information, including the rifle settings and the look and feel of your general position. Get out of position and take a break for a couple of minutes. Get back into position to see whether you can repeat what the setup position felt like. Does the gun settle back in the same place? Does it want to stay in the position or drift away? Do this three or four times per position.

Even after you have been shooting for a few months, practice this drill. When you set out to shoot 100 training shots in one position, you know that you'll be taking breaks. Decide when to take them, develop a strategy for getting good shots off when your position feels great, and decide when you're going to get out of your position when it, and therefore your hold, starts to break down.

Prematch Drill 2.   *Line Exercise*

When your position is solid and repeatable, you need to learn to adjust it around the target. This easy exercise helps you practice adjusting. On the back of a target, draw three black vertical lines that run from the top of the target to the bottom (figure 9.4). Make them about as wide as one bull. Hang this target.

Each line should be the width of the target. Set up your position so that you are naturally pointed at the left line. Raise your rifle into position five times, holding on the line for 8 to 10 seconds each time. This is about the length of time that you'd take to shoot one shot. Try to get your rifle to settle down on the line, keeping right and left movement as small as possible. On the fourth repetition, check your natural point of aim (NPA) to see whether you are still naturally pointed at the line.

Shift your position to the centerline. Check your NPA to see whether you've moved enough. Repeat the five-holds drill. Repeat, using the line on the right. Shift your position all the way back to the left line and find your NPA one more time.

This drill teaches hold control, focus, NPA shift, and consistency. You also learn the movement required to shift your body from one row of bulls to the next and the importance of rechecking NPA. For beginning shooters, NPA can shift and settle even when they are aiming at the same location. As you progress in the sport, you'll be more consistent as your positions strengthen and feel

Figure 9.4 Draw three vertical lines on the back of a paper target.

more natural. But even advanced shooters need to check NPA regularly while shooting a whole match at one single-bull location.

Prematch Drill 3.   *Group Shooting*

This exercise helps you work on positions, build consistency, adjust sights, and identify the elements that go into your shot plan. When you sight in for a match, you start by group shooting. Practice this now at all the bulls on the target to develop endurance in the shooting position and focus for taking shots.

The two center bulls on the target are your sighting bulls. You will always start shooting at these first, so practice setting up on one of those as you establish your sighting-in routine. Set your NPA and get ready to sight in. Take three to five shots to evaluate where the rifle is shooting. You don't even have to look at these shots; pay attention to your NPA, and follow-through and warm up your body and position.

After shooting three to five shots, look through the scope to see whether you've shot a group. If so, click your sights to move the center of the group to the center of the bull. If you haven't shot a group, check NPA again and make sure that your follow-through is staying on target and that your position feels settled. If any of those elements are out of adjustment, fix them before clicking your sights.

When you are consistent and on target, pay attention to your shots and see whether you can call shot location. If you can, move your shots into the center of the target as you continue sighting in. If your shots are not on call, keep shooting until you have a group and then adjust it to the center of the bull. A beginning shooter may need to use both bulls to get sighted in. The goal is to get all larger adjustments done on one bull so that you are calling good shots and they are going where you think that they should go. Use the second sighting bull to refine your timing and shot plan to simulate what you want to do in a match. Whether in a match or at practice, try to sight in like this consistently to perfect your sighting-in plan. You will know when you are ready to go for record.

In this exercise, you go for record just as you would for any target, but you continue to shoot three to five shots at each bull on the target. You'll notice if NPA is not correct because the whole group will be off center. This exercise is effective because it lets you shoot a series of shots at one bull without having to readjust NPA for each shot to see whether your position and timing are consistent. Trying to get the group size smaller as you progress is fun as well. This exercise eliminates changing targets after every 10 or 20 shots, so work on building endurance as you repeat shots at each bull.

As you perform this drill you will see that after you adjust NPA at a new target, it can stay there for the rest of the shots. The drill may show that you aren't moving enough or that you change position when you move in a way that decreases stability. If you shoot one or two targets using this drill every day in the prematch phase, you will be well on your way to understanding NPA adjustment, stability, and position repeatability, and you will gain concentration skills to boot.

Prematch Drill 4. *Dry Firing and Holding*

This exercise is similar to the line exercise except that you now hold on a bull and go through the motions of taking a shot but without loading the rifle. Your rifle will likely have a dry-firing switch on it that you should engage so that you don't damage any of the components of the rifle while practicing.

You can practice dry firing at home or on the range whenever you want to focus on position to work out any balance or rifle issues before you start shooting. Some shooters think that they can work out balance issues while shooting, but they become frustrated when shots go wide because of a poor hold, which results from poor balance and positioning. You nip this chain reaction in the bud if you work on the source.

To practice dry firing and holding at home, place a smaller target on the wall. Try to make it look like a normal target that you see through your sights at the range. The black on this training bull may be only 0.5 inch (1.25 cm) in diameter so that it looks like a regular air rifle target in your front sight.

Try a variety of training techniques. Dry-fire without wearing your jacket for a while. Dry-fire without wearing your boots or your shooting pants. Using these variations will make your body work harder to achieve balance and stability. Although you will never shoot at a match without shooting gear on, training in this way pushes your body to its limits to build balance and stamina. The brain assesses balance based on information coming from the eyes and feet. Requiring the body to send and evaluate more of this type of information will speed up the process of developing balance in position, leading to a better hold. The first goal is to get the smallest hold possible before taking shots. Dry firing and holding exercises will get you there faster.

For holding exercises, place a clock with a second hand where you can see it. You may want to place it at your side so that you can look at it even when holding the rifle. In standing position and with the rifle on the rest, pick up the rifle as you would for a normal shot and look through the sights. Hold this position for 20 to 30 seconds, depending on your stamina. Take a number of breaths during the hold phase but try to use breath control as you would for a normal shot. Work to get your hold as small as possible each time you stop your breath. You may get three holds in for each 20- or 30-second phase. When the time is up, set down the rifle and rest for 20 to 30 seconds. Repeat this exercise for 15 minutes at first; work up to 30 minutes. If you are dry firing with different gear removed, pay attention to how your body feels. Don't overdo it if you become tense or tired. Shooting without the jacket really works the back. Be sure to build up to a number of holds before you go for longer periods. You want your body to feel tired as you build stamina, but stop before the fatigue that you feel becomes pain. Work up to 30 minutes with three variations of shooter gear (no jacket, no boots, or no shooting pants).

If you can't get to the range more than three times a week, performing holding and dry-firing exercises a couple of days a week at home can add a lot of points to your score. These exercises help develop muscle memory of positions and will shrink your hold faster than any other training method will. You can also work on timing to learn to take shots on the inside of your hold pattern and ideally over the center of the target.

Shot Plans

Now that you are shooting and working on each of the elements that go into a shot, increase your accuracy and ability to account for all the factors that you need to focus on for each shot by building a shot plan. A shot plan encompasses the time from the evaluation of your last shot through the calling of your current shot.

In the prematch phase of training, focus is on the physical aspects of taking the shot. As you progress, you will add more mental aspects as they make sense and as you can apply them to your whole shot process. A shot plan for a beginning shooter at the prematch phase might look like this:

1. Check that the last shot was on call.
2. Load the rifle and relax the mind and body.
3. Bring the rifle up and check NPA.
4. Check that NPA is adjusted and on the new target.
5. Check rear and front sight alignment.
6. Take three breaths that cross over the bull.
7. Stop the last breath half to three-fourths of the way so that sights are on the bull.
8. Let the hold settle over the center of the bull.
9. Squeeze the trigger while staying centered.
10. Follow through for one to two seconds over the bull so that nothing disturbs the shot.
11. Call the shot location.

You should account for these basic shot plan elements in each shot until they become second nature. Poor shots occur when you forget or ignore one or more of these elements. You can readily identify where you need to improve in your shot process if you have identified each element going into the shot.

Mental Game Plan

At this stage, point gains come from actual training and shooting. The mental game plan for the prematch phase focuses on identifying a mental blueprint of the perfect shot and discovering the mind-set in which you perform well. Start to think about the big picture. Think about the days when you performed well and remember what you said to yourself while shooting. Think about the attitude that you had that day going into training or the match. Think about the things that you controlled and your focus. Take notes so that you can evaluate other days that go well. Perhaps you'll notice a pattern and be able to identify mental items that you want to account for each time you shoot. This process is the start to identifying the mind-set that leads to successful matches.

Now think about days when you didn't perform well. Ask yourself the same kinds of questions. What was your attitude that day? Did something distract you? What were you saying to yourself? If you notice a pattern, perhaps you can change something before you start shooting to get the most out of your training or match.

Mental training can help you overcome things that led to poor shooting in the past. What is important now is to identify the attitudes, motivation, self-talk, and possible distractions to work on in the future. Learn to repeat the good things and change or eliminate the bad from your mental blueprint and mind-set.

Competition Phase

After the prematch phase, your positions should come more easily and more consistently. Now when you assume a position, you probably know immediately that something is out of place or that the angles are wrong, and you can correct it without losing time and energy. Many beginning shooters don't notice things that are out of place, and they keep shooting. At the end, they wonder why their shots were off call or why their position didn't settle only to find that their cheek piece or sights were in the wrong location or that their feet were sinking off the edge of the kneeling roll. You should now notice problems like this right away and not struggle so much to figure out what is happening. In this phase, you really benefit from your previous hard work and your scores will start to rise.

The physical side of training includes position work with more of a match focus. Shift your emphasis from working on stability, balance, and endurance to thinking about getting shots off when hold and timing are at their peak. You still want to get rounds down range, practicing at least two positions per training session, but shift your focus away from what is happening in your body to what the sight picture looks like and what your recoil and follow-through are telling you.

Practice Drills

In contrast to the internal and position-focused drills in the prematch phase, drills in the competition phase deal with shooting good shots, learning to recover, and pressing on to end strong. These drills introduce components of mental toughness and have a goal-oriented structure.

Individual Competition Drill 1.   Start-Middle-Finish

For this drill, shoot your first 20 shots for the day as you would a match. Get in position, get sighted in, and go for record for 20 shots. Have your coach score. Take 30 to 60 shots of training and then shoot another 20 shots for record and score.

This drill highlights a couple of things. The first practice match requires you to be ready to shoot right from the start as you would in a real match.

In the second practice match you must take your focus back to match conditions and reestablish your competitive mind-set. The drill also shows how your endurance and concentration hold up after training. If you score significantly higher in either of the two practice matches, analyze why and see whether you can apply your strategies on match day.

Individual Competition Drill 2.   String of 10s

While training, see how many 10s you can shoot in a row. After you establish a number, try to beat it.

This drill builds confidence and drive to continue to improve.

Individual Competition Drill 3.   Number of 10s in 60 Shots

For this drill, instead of just setting out to shoot 60 training shots, try to get as many 10s as you can in those 60 shots. Don't count any score other than a 10. Do this every few weeks to see whether your numbers increase. At first, you may shoot only 20 10s in 60 shots, but by the end of the season, that number may be up to 40!

Individual Competition Drill 4.   Ten 10s

Shoot one 10-bull target. Keep shooting at a bull until you have a 10 and then move on to the next bull. Count how many shots it takes to shoot the whole target. Your goal is to lower that number each time you shoot. When you add the penalty of having to stay on a target until you shoot a good shot, you introduce a factor of pressure. Learn to deal with pressure in training so that in a match you'll know how to act and react.

Individual Competition Drill 5. *Blast-Off*

Shoot a more challenging position for this drill. If you constantly shoot 10s in a position that you like, such as prone, the drill will not provide enough challenge.

After you get sighted in, start on the bottom left-hand bull. Your goal is to climb to the upper right-hand bull during the exercise, where you get to blast off the target. Progress to the next bull only if you shoot a 10. If you shoot a 9, you have to go back one bull. If you shoot an 8, you have to go back two bulls and start again. Your goal is to get to the top right bull in as few shots as possible, using the fewest bulls.

This drill teaches you how to deal with successful and unsuccessful shots. You will feel the pressure of each 8 or 9, but you will also feel the pressure on the second-to-last bull with just one shot to go until you can blast off the target with a 10.

You can also use this exercise to compete with your teammates. Don't set a time limit. Have everyone get sighted in (you don't have to use the same position) and progress through the exercise at your own pace. When everyone has blasted off, have the coach count the number of shots and the number of bulls that each shooter used. The shooter with the fewest is declared the winner.

Team Competition Drill 1. *Climb the Mountain*

In this drill you have five sets or more of five-shot strings, depending on time and the number of shooters. The coach ranks shooters based on estimated lowest to highest averages on a sheet (lowest at the top of the list, highest at the bottom). You are competing only against the shooters just above and just below you. Everyone shoots his or her first five shots for a total score. If you beat the shooter above you, you move up one place. If you don't beat the shooter above you and the shooter below you beats your score, you move down one place. If you have the lowest score of all shooters, you drop to the bottom of the list. You can move up only one place at a time (for one set of five shots) and only if you beat the person above you. If the person above you didn't

beat the person above her or him but beats you, the rank stays the same and the person with the lowest score drops to the bottom. The goal is to keep climbing. After you make it to the top, try to maintain your position by continuing to beat the person just below you.

This drill brings out some intense shooting and creates excitement after each five-shot string. It helps you learn to deal with the pressure of competition. Finals shooting is similar to this, but instead of five-shot strings, you are scored after each shot. This drill is a good endurance builder for intensity. You learn what it is like to have your score announced and how to deal with either climbing or descending the mountain of shooters.

Team Competition Drill 2. *Practice Matches*

Try to have a practice match with the whole team whenever you can. If you have only a few days of practice each week, you may be able to have a practice match only every other week. If you have the days to do it, have a practice match every week. If you train on your own most of the time, schedule two to four practice matches a month that you train and prepare for just as you do a regular match. Run the practice match exactly like

a regular match so that you are prepared for time restrictions, position changeovers, and the time limits for each position. Keep track of your scores for these matches just as you do your regular match scores and see how they compare. Your coach may want to create a wall chart to keep track of scores so that all shooters can see how they progress over the season.

Team Competition Drill 3.   *Finals Training*

Larger matches, including most national championships, include a final. You should add finals into your training early in the competition phase. The whole shooting line can practice finals. Practice finals from the standing position.

Have a coach or line officer call commands and keep score. If you are training on paper targets, each shooter can call off her or his own score to save time. Have someone add up scores so that after at least 5, 9, and 10 shots, the scores can be announced so that all shooters know where they stand in the match.

The rules and commands for shooting a final follow. The shooters can be on their practice points and in random order. To have a more realistic finals practice, shooters can line up in rank according to practice match scores.

- "Your three-minute preparation period begins now." You can handle your rifle, establish NPA, and do holding exercises.

- "Five-minute sighting-in period. Start." You have unlimited sighting shots during this time.

- "30 seconds." Oral warning that the sighting period ends in 30 seconds and that you must clear your barrel of any remaining shots.

- "Stop." Stop shooting. If you still have a round in the barrel, notify the range officer or coach. During training, you will just shoot it down range off your target. In a match, you will have to clear it in a special shot container or backstop. A 30-second pause is given before the next command. This is not stated aloud to the shooters; time simply elapses.

- "For the first shot, load." The line officer will say, "For your next shot, load," on all the remaining shots in the final.

- "Attention, 3-2-1. Start." You have 75 seconds to shoot your shot.

- "Stop."

- "Results of the first shot. Position 1." The shooter calls out his or her score. The line officer calls, "Position 2," and so on down the line until all shooters have called out their scores.

- "Totals after five shots are position 1 [score], position 2 [score]" and so on down the line. The coach or line officer who is keeping track calls this.

- "Final results are position 1 (score), position 2 (score)," and so on down the line until all scores are announced.

Add variations to your finals training as well:

- Allow only 45 seconds, instead of 75, to take a shot.

- Require yourself to put down the rifle at least once during the 75 seconds without taking the shot. Then you have to pick it up again, get settled, and take the shot with less time. This exercise teaches you that you really have enough time to take a second or third hold if the first one doesn't look or feel right.

- Have other noises and distractions going on while you are concentrating on taking the shot. This exercise helps you learn to block out distractions that can take you away from the task at hand.

- Have a "guts match." This is where the shooter with the lowest score has to sit down. If there is a tie for the lowest score, have a shoot-off to determine who is eliminated. It gets exciting when you're one of the last two shooters on the line in a sudden death elimination to determine the winner. Each shot is taken under the same "finals" format.

Shot Plans

In the competition phase, you advance to using both physical and mental cues in the shot plan. As you gain more control of positions and timing, advance your shot plan so that the physical characteristics come more automatically, freeing you to focus on the mental aspects that help you shoot better shots.

A shot plan at the competition stage may look something like this:

1. Check that the last shot was on call.
2. Calm your mind. Mentally rehearse the perfect shot blueprint.
3. Bring up your rifle and check NPA. Check for any tension in your body.
4. Check that NPA is correct. Dry-fire a perfect shot.
5. Load and bring up the rifle for a shot.
6. Close your eyes and feel your position settle. Breathe out any tension.
7. Practice breath control so that your last breath ends with a perfect sight picture.
8. Check rear- and front-sight alignment.
9. Focus on the bull. Wait for your hold to settle.
10. Squeeze the shot while aiming inside of a good hold.
11. Follow through and keep looking at the bull past the shot.
12. Call the shot.

Mental Game Plan

Now that you know the mental state in which you perform well, you need to create this state and work within it. You know whether you perform better when calm or fired up, when totally focused, or when following a specific checklist of tasks. The next step covers strategies to maximize the mental state in which you like to perform. Through the competition practice drills, you will learn a lot about yourself and your handling of shooting situations. Try various mind-sets to see whether they help you recover faster from a challenge. Keep in mind that our sport is all about staying calm, cool, and collected under challenges and shooting successful shots through them. Track in your journal what you think and say to yourself during these challenges. Identify the words, thoughts, and feelings that either helped you or hurt you and repeat the good things or eliminate the bad from your mental game plan.

Championship Phase

Congratulations on working hard to get through the first two physical phases of the season. The championship phase focuses on quality shooting and lets up on quantity. Ideally, by this stage your positions are solid and consistent, and you feel very much in control. Your mental perspective has shifted from thinking primarily about making your body still (what is going on behind the firing line) to thinking primarily about shooting a 10 (what is on the target). Training and tasks need to replicate the championship environment closely so that you can face that challenge consistently and be ready for the big day.

During range training, shoot targets as you would in a match. Because you have only 20 shots to do your job, think of training in the same perspective and increase the demands of quality in fewer shots. In previous phases, training focused on getting many shots down range, and you could see that maybe the third, fifth, and eighth series were pretty good. In this phase, you don't have all those series or targets to see how well you can shoot. You need to shoot well when it counts, so train that way. Set up a couple of 20-shot series and practice them in the time and structure of a match. Move on to the next position and do the same. The focus is on handling quality shooting in those 20 shots. You can't say, "I'll try harder next time" or "I wasn't ready to go for record." You have to practice putting it on the line and performing to your full potential when it counts. Make training count.

Practice Drills

Drills now focus on challenging match conditions as well as some fun team activities to mix things up a bit.

Individual Championship Drill 1. *Speed Drill*

Perform this drill from standing or kneeling position. This drill mimics what it is like to be low on time with shots to go. Set three periods to get off 10 shots. The first period is 10 minutes, the second is 5 minutes, and the third is 3 minutes. Total up all three 10-shot rounds and see whether your score improves the next time you run the drill. You may find that the 3-minute target score is higher than the 10-minute score. This result may tell you something about trusting your shot and taking the 10 when you see it.

Do this drill only after your positions and shot plan are solid. A beginning shooter who tries to do this kind of drill will likely reinforce bad habits and become confused. This drill shows you that you can still follow and rely on your shot plan, even with 10 shots to go in three minutes.

Individual Championship Drill 2. *Get to 40*

See how many shots it takes you to you get 40 10s. Try to beat this number in subsequent training sessions.

Individual Championship Drill 3. *Positive Versus Negative*

This drill helps build mental toughness and focus. In general, it will help you turn negative thinking into positive thinking. You will learn to recognize negative self-talk and understand what it can do to your performance.

In the first part of the drill, think positively about shooting as many 10s as you can in 10 shots. Don't worry about time or shooting strings. Take one good shot after another and see how many 10s you get. In this part of the drill, you are set up to go for a 10 on each shot (a positive approach). Count the number of 10s that you shot.

In the next part of the drill, shoot as many shots as you can (up to 10 shots) until you shoot a 9. After you shoot a 9 (or lower), this part is over.

Again, count the number of shots. How does this number compare with the number that you shot in the first part? The goal of the drill is to help you overcome worrying about the possibility of shooting a poor shot. In the second part of the drill, you are set up to try not to shoot a 9 (a negative approach). In the second part of the drill, if you change your focus for each shot from avoiding a 9 to "What does it take for me to shoot one successful shot?" and follow your shot plan, you'll teach yourself to refocus when doubt comes into your mind. In the negative part of the drill, your self-talk was "Don't shoot a 9." After practicing to change your self-talk, you'll get back to a positive mind-set in which you're going after the 10s.

Team Championship Drill 1. *Save Your Teammate*

You can do this drill after a regular finals training drill. It is run just like a final—one shot at a time. The goal is to save as many of your teammates as possible by keeping them in the game. The teammate who needs to be saved is the one with the lowest shot on the line. The teammate to the right of that shooter must shoot a 10 alone and under the regular finals format to save the teammate and keep her or him in the game. If the shooter scores anything less than a 10, the original shooter with the lowest score is out. The coach running the game can pick a certain number of saves, such as half the number of shooters, for the team as a whole to win the game.

This drill teaches focus under challenging circumstances. You are not only shooting a single shot by yourself with the whole team watching but also feeling the pressure to save your teammate to help win the game.

Team Championship Drill 2. *Team Externals Match*

For this drill, split the team into two groups. While one group shoots a final or 10-shot string, the other group can talk, bother, yell, or do whatever they want to distract the shooters. The distractors are not allowed to touch the shooters or physically change their positions while bothering them. All targets are added up for a team total. Switch sides so that the shooting team gets to disturb the other team while they try to shoot. Run the drill like a final or set a time limit for a string of 10 shots. All targets count toward the team score. This drill helps improve your concentration when you feel singled out by competitors who are out to get you. Any match will seem calm and tranquil after this experience. Your job is to shoot good shots through the mayhem.

Team Championship Drill 3. *10s Relay*

This speed drill is a fun activity to end practice. At the end of practice, when everyone is mentally and physically drained from working hard, start with the shooter on the far left. When that person shoots a 10, he or she can stop. The shooter to the person's right then has to shoot until she or he shoots a 10, and so on down the line. This keeps going until everyone on the line shoots a 10 as his or her final shot of the day. Then everyone can pack up and go home. Pressure starts to build after three or four shots, not only because people want to get going but also because you are shooting with everyone watching and you need to perform even when you're tired.

Team Championship Drill 4. *Tennis Match*

In this drill, two shooters pair off and shoot a tennis match. After each shooter shoots one shot, the winner of that round gets the points. Score it like a tennis match of 15, 30, 40, and 45 to win on the fourth round. For deuce (a tie at 40), shooters need to continue to shoot until someone wins by two rounds (or shots in this case). When someone is eliminated, two winners from the first set shoot another tennis match to see who will go on to the finals or the next set. Get down to the top two shooters. The eliminated players cheer and clap as the top two shooters fight for the last round.

Shot Plans

As you progress in shooting, your shot plans will become more automatic—less of a checklist and more of an awareness plan. When your shot blueprint is routine and consistent, an item that is out of place is more likely to come to your attention. This progression is natural and desired. You want to have your focus and energy on the areas that need attention. You learn to trust yourself to notice when something is wrong or out of place and to correct it before taking the shot. When you are struggling or are not able to call your shots, you may want to revert to the checklist shot plan to account for everything. When shooting at a high level, focus, intensity, stress, and mind-set are more a part of the shot plan than are the actual steps for taking a shot. A shot plan at this level may look something like this:

1. Check that the last shot was on call.

2. Breathe and relax.

3. Mentally load the image of the perfect sight picture. See the sharp lines and when to react to it. Say cue words to help with focus and determination to get into the 10 ring.

4. Raise the rifle and get ready. Close your eyes and mentally scan your body to see that everything is relaxed and ready to go. Open your eyes and check NPA.

5. Breathing is automatic and stops over the 10 ring.

6. Hold settles. Anticipate the sights going into the 10 ring and act on that anticipation. Be proactive with the shot and let it happen when it's right.

7. Evaluate the recoil (if there is any movement) and follow-through, what clues they give about timing, whether too fast or too slow.

8. Call the shot.

9. If on call, load the same image and anticipation plan. If off call, assess the length of the hold and the timing of the shot. Load the new image and timing plan to improve the shot.

10. Repeat.

Mental Game Plan

The shot plan is part of a larger overall competition plan. Check and control your energy level, self-talk, focus, and other mental elements that can either help or hurt performance. Negative self-talk between shots will affect your performance. Awareness picks up that this needs to be corrected, and you go into your refocus routine. (The refocus routine will be discussed in more depth in the next step.) In this phase, the mental game plan is in effect the whole time that you are shooting. Notice where your mind goes and whether or not that place or thinking is helpful or harmful to performance. Dwelling on poor shots will have a certain effect, and anticipating a great shot will have another. Now that you've advanced to the point that your mind isn't filled with just the physical mechanics of shooting, it is freer to attend to more complex issues.

SUCCESS SUMMARY OF PRACTICING FOR OPTIMAL PERFORMANCE

Step 9 has helped you move from a beginning shooter to an experienced one. As your shot plan becomes more efficient and automatic, you can put your experiences to use to help you adjust your plan for better performance. The drills in this step have moved from simple to complex, dealing first with positions and physical assessment and later to turning negative thinking around to help you on the next shot. Add your own variations to the drills to make them more challenging and fun throughout the season. One thing is for sure—the need for training and drills will continue season to season.

What will probably always change is your mental game plan for the big picture. As you continue in the sport, your mental game plan will evolve as you find new ways to bring out the best in yourself and motivate yourself to keep going. Few people reach their full potential. Those who can apply what they learn in their shooting to other areas of their lives gain the most from their time in the sport and their mental game plans.

Before Taking the Next Step

Before moving on to step 10, Training Mentally and Physically, evaluate what you have learned to this point. Answer each of the following questions honestly. If you are able to answer all six questions, you are ready to move on to the next step.

1. Have you set up your shooter's journal?
2. Have you built a shot plan that addresses what you need to check to shoot one successful shot?
3. Have you drilled getting in and out of position so that you know that your position is solid and repeatable?
4. Have you set up a dry-firing range at home?
5. Do you have practice matches scheduled in your season plan?
6. Have you designated a match at the end of your season to be your championship match in which you will strive to perform your best?

Training Mentally and Physically

Shooting is a mental sport. After you establish your positions and stability, get your hold under control, sharpen your timing, and perfect your ability to call shots, success comes down to being mentally strong enough to manage the conditions of the day so that you can perform to your full potential. Other shooters will see the scores that you shoot in a match and compare them to their own. You need to develop the mind-set to deal with this challenge. Instead of being uncomfortable that your scores will be posted, change your attitude so that you can't wait to show what you've got. To do this in a strategic and realistic way, you need to set goals.

SETTING GOALS

Goal setting is the strongest and most effective mental strategy you can use throughout your shooting career. Goals are the reason that we participate in an activity. Your goal may be simply to have fun, to become a stronger competitor under pressure, to earn a college scholarship, or to make the Olympic team. Your goals motivate you toward action and keep you on the journey until you reach your destination.

Long-Term Goals

Think about where you want to be in 2, 3, 4, or 10 years. This is your long-term goal. (See the examples in figure 10.1.) Some people are called to be doctors, athletes, military personnel, or to take over the family business. These deep beliefs determine drive and direction until a person accomplishes that goal. Not everyone has this sense of direction, and that's fine, too. Maybe you need to keep searching until you find the sport or activity that inspires and motivates you to participate and excel. People are cut out for different things in life, and you need to find what grabs hold of your imagination and becomes an aspiration. You will know when you have found an activity that you will enjoy for a long time because it teaches you the things that you most want to learn. When you discover your passion, you need to map out where you want to take the activity and how long you'll need to get there.

Goals are part of mental strategy because they help develop perspective. Goals help you realistically examine where you are now, where you

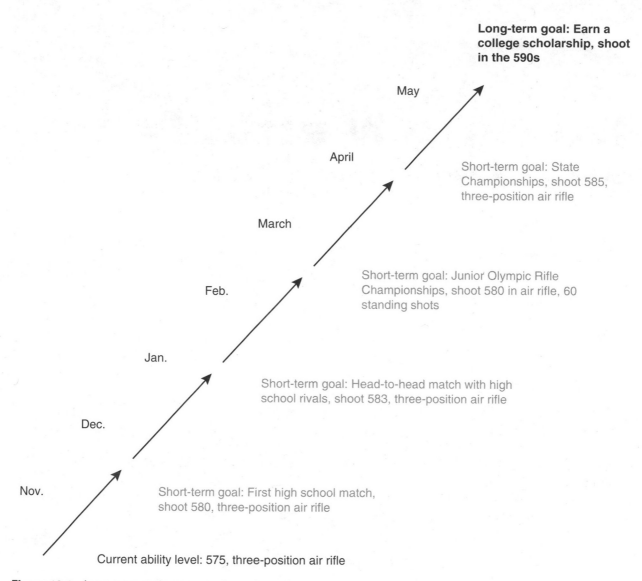

Long-term goal: Earn a college scholarship, shoot in the 590s

May

April

Short-term goal: State Championships, shoot 585, three-position air rifle

March

Feb.

Short-term goal: Junior Olympic Rifle Championships, shoot 580 in air rifle, 60 standing shots

Jan.

Short-term goal: Head-to-head match with high school rivals, shoot 583, three-position air rifle

Dec.

Nov.

Short-term goal: First high school match, shoot 580, three-position air rifle

Current ability level: 575, three-position air rifle

Figure 10.1 Long-term goals on a sample road map to success.

want to go in the future, how long it will take to get to higher levels, and what you need to do to get there. Without this road map of direction and time, you can easily become lost during all the hours, days, weeks, and months of training. You may become frustrated if you are not improving as quickly as you would like, or setbacks may diminish your motivation. A clear road map of your journey and an understanding that each new level takes longer to achieve will keep you on track. Use the challenging times to prove to yourself that you can overcome obstacles and become stronger for surmounting them.

Long-term goals are the destination of your road map. Establish a timeline. At the end of the

timeline, write your long-term goals. You may be looking years down the road. The point is that anything worth working for is going to take some time. If it comes too easily to you, you may lose motivation and determination because you didn't have to work to earn it.

After you have established long-term goals and placed them on the timeline at the correct dates—for example, earning a shooting scholarship your freshman year of college or earning a spot on the U.S. National Development Team at certain matches in the upcoming year—add specific performance information that will move you toward accomplishing those goals. For example, imagine that winning a college scholarship is your long-term goal. College coaches look at scores and match performances to gauge a prospect's ability level, to determine whether that shooter could make their team, and to decide how much scholarship money they will offer the shooter if she or he is within range of being on the team. You need to find out what other shooters at the college level are shooting and set your goals accordingly. To get the right perspective when setting goals, consider how much time you have to reach that level. A high school senior who tries to add 50 points to his or her score to get within range of a goal started too late. The student will have to change perspective, readjust goals, and work toward something more realistic.

As another example, imagine that making the National Development Team (NDT) is your goal. Find out what scores it took to make the team the last few years and set your goals accordingly. If you are 30 points off, you will need a couple of years to reach that competitive level. If you are 15 points off, it will take a year or so. If you are 5 points off, you are within striking distance. Keep up the great work and go for it.

Long-term goals set the timeline and can be specific about the performance level required to accomplish them. Now you know where you want to go and what it's going to take to get you there. Establishing this timeline reinforces the right perspective. You are not just hoping and wishing that you can make it; you know what it takes. Continue to gauge your progress to see whether you're on track.

Short-Term Goals

Short-term goals can cover one, two, four, or six months, depending on the goal. (See figure 10.2 for sample short-term goals.) If your long-term goal is to qualify for the Olympic Games, you have four or eight years to divide into short-term goal periods. Each segment may be six months long. If you have an important last match of the season coming up in two months, you may measure short-term goals in weekly segments. Short-term goals are checkpoints that you set for yourself to measure your current ability level.

They will likely coincide with the important matches that you shoot throughout the year, and they provide a perfect way to evaluate your current ability level.

To set short-term goals, review your long-term goal and work backward. Write in all the matches or important dates that you will use to evaluate your ability level. Space out the dates so that you can focus on different factors in training over time before you evaluate that training through performance. Write your current ability level at the beginning of your road map. Think about where you are and where you want to go, and evaluate whether that rate of growth is realistic. A beginning shooter can gain 100 points a year. But keep in mind that the higher your scores go, the longer it will take to raise your average. Top shooters are thrilled if they raise their averages 3 points a year. They push the maximum amount of points possible just about every time they shoot, so a 3-point increase is huge. Scoring goals also need to be based on how much time you have to devote to training and how often you can compete. Someone who competes often will likely have a higher average because one poor performance won't have a large effect. Someone who competes only a couple of times a year can set goals for an average but shouldn't let that average alone define her or his ability level.

Short-term goals need to be measurable and specific, relate to performance, and be spaced out so that you can determine whether the way that you are training is having the desired effect. Identify the events that you want to use for short-term goals but wait until a few weeks before the event to write down the scores that you would like to shoot. If you write them down too early and they are far above or below your ability level at the event, you will set yourself up for frustration or lack of motivation. Write down a score range of 3 to 10 points, depending on how consistent you are and your ability level. For a beginning shooter, a score range of 530 to 540 points is a realistic and challenging goal. Set your goals at least to the level that you have shot in the past and slightly higher. Setting your goal 20 points higher than you have

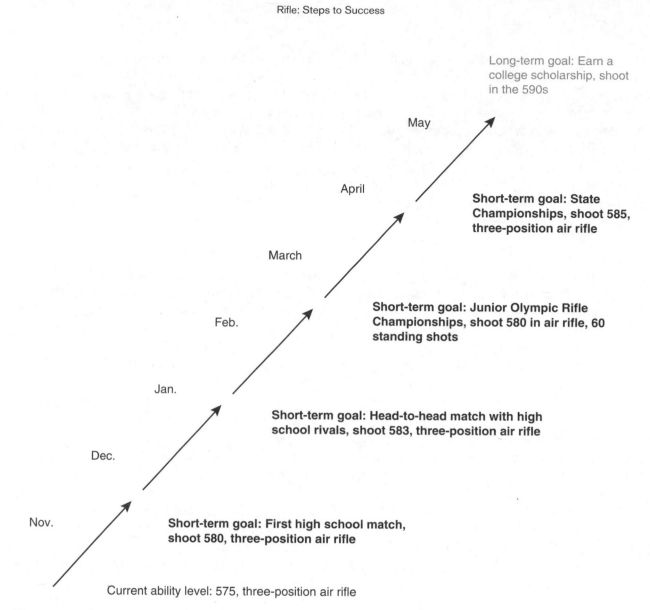

Long-term goal: Earn a college scholarship, shoot in the 590s

May

April

Short-term goal: State Championships, shoot 585, three-position air rifle

March

Short-term goal: Junior Olympic Rifle Championships, shoot 580 in air rifle, 60 standing shots

Feb.

Jan.

Short-term goal: Head-to-head match with high school rivals, shoot 583, three-position air rifle

Dec.

Nov.

Short-term goal: First high school match, shoot 580, three-position air rifle

Current ability level: 575, three-position air rifle

Figure 10.2   Short-term goals on a sample road map to success.

ever shot is not realistic and will set you up for failure. Even if you need to shoot that score to have a chance of winning a match, you should set goals that just push your ability level. Do not set goals that are too easy or too hard. Goals reflect your performance, not the performances of your competitors. Focus on what it takes for you to shoot a great personal score, not the score that you think others shoot. You don't have any control over what others shoot, so don't waste energy worrying about that. Put energy into the elements of your performance that you can control to reach a goal that means something to you. Learning to focus this way through goal

setting will help you develop mental discipline for a long time to come.

Biweekly, Weekly, and Daily Goals

An example of biweekly goals was shown in step 9. Some shooters write weekly and daily goals in their performance journals almost daily. Focus these goals on specific training techniques and tasks to work on. At the beginning of each week or at the end of a week's training segment (say on Friday afternoon), identify three areas—from among such areas as hold control, trigger control, follow-through, shot calling, emotion control, shot plan, or finals training—to work on during the next training segment. You may work on a specific task for weeks until you have it under control so that it helps performance. You may work on another task for only one week because you know from experience that if you focus on this item right before the match, you gain confidence. Weekly and daily goals are the workhorses of goal setting. Although long- and short-term goals focus on outcomes, such as making a team or shooting in a specific score range, weekly and daily goals are performance goals that focus on the specific tasks required for accomplishing various aspects of performance. Unlike goals in which the outcome is not always within your control, performance goals are completely within your control and can help build confidence and consistency. These are the factors that you concentrate on in practice and learn to rely on in a match. They include each aspect of your shot plan and the way that you put them together to work best. When all else fails, go back to focusing on specific tasks. The rest will fall into place because of repetition and consistency in training.

We have worked from the largest to the smallest building blocks to assemble a goal-setting road map. By working from the largest perspective to the smallest, the daily goals have a place in the overall scheme. Daily goals are the small stepping-stones that will get you where you want to go. When you have a road map in place that includes realistic and challenging long- and short-term goals, you are on your way to becoming a confident and motivated shooter.

BUILDING AND MANAGING SELF-CONFIDENCE

Self-confidence is the realistic belief that you are capable of accomplishing the task at hand. When you think about an upcoming match, do you feel confident that you can achieve your goals and shoot at a level that coincides with your training scores? If you do, then you have self-confidence. For shooters, the task at hand is the next match, the next position, the next set of 10 shots, the next individual shot. When broken down like this, the task becomes manageable and controllable. Having a plan for each step in the process enhances self-confidence, which comes from training correctly, gaining match experience, and developing a focused plan that helps you perform to your full potential.

Many athletes have a misconception that self-confidence is what it takes to win, that if they go into a competition absolutely confident that they will defeat the opponent, they will do it. If it were that easy, competition wouldn't be necessary. Winners could be declared by judging who is the most confident. Luckily, competition is more than that. It comes down to the overall performance, which includes managing and believing in yourself, to determine who wins.

When athletes use self-confidence to focus only on winning, they develop a habit of evaluating performance based only on outcome and not on the elements within their control. Athletes who focus only on winning fall into a trap of overconfidence or cockiness. These athletes talk the talk but can't walk the walk. Acting overconfident is really a cover-up to hide insecurity. Cockiness may be all that they have to show that they are competitive and really want to win. After the competition begins and their performance doesn't back up all the hype, these athletes fall quickly and often perform far below their ability level. You should avoid acting overconfident even if others are or because you think that you need to psych out your opponents. You are falsely lifting yourself up. If you don't have realistic performance goals to hold yourself up, you will crash back to reality with a major letdown. Let your scores speak for themselves in competition. Do not let your ego get ahead of itself.

At times you may feel overconfident because your scores are way ahead of the competition. If this is the case and you are less motivated because the match doesn't seem that hard, look up your long-term goals again. Think about where you want to be at the end of the season. Think about the kind of scores you will need. You don't want to waste a competitive opportunity. Raise the bar for yourself. Instead of thinking, "I need to shoot at this lower level to win this match" (and trust me, you will shoot at this lower level if you don't change your mind-set), think about replicating the main match that you are working toward that year. Lay it all on the line and see how close you are to shooting the scores that you will need to accomplish your season-ending goal. Learn to challenge yourself and create the kind of competition that you need to succeed long term. You will be well on your way to mental toughness.

Athletes often face confidence problems, usually low self-confidence or the feeling that their true ability isn't high enough to prevail over the task at hand. These problems can be devastating. Often they come about over time because of negative feedback from parents or coaches, a focus only on winning, unrealistic goals set by others, self-doubt in their abilities, lack of training, fear of failure, negative images of themselves, a tendency to be easily intimidated, or feelings of anxiety and low self-image. It takes time for athletes to lose their self-confidence, and it will take some time to undo the damage and regain it.

The key is to prevent this downward spiral from the beginning. Feeling a little doubt or worry can be constructive for some athletes because it fuels motivation and raises the desire to succeed in the face of challenge. The problem occurs when doubt and worry become destructive and start to affect self-confidence, self-worth, and performance. Identifying when doubt and worry have a negative effect on performance is critical. Some athletes continue to think that their ability level is simply poor and that they aren't competitive or worthy. They begin to ride that downward spiral. They need to see that the doubt and worry are affecting their ability level and that they have it within their control to lessen the effect or eliminate it altogether.

Goals to Build Self-Confidence

You can always rely on your goals. As discussed earlier, when you set realistic yet challenging goals for yourself, you can go into a competition with excitement and confidence. You know that you have shot close to your goal in the past and that the training you completed should propel you to the higher end of your goal range. Goals can be the foundation to self-confidence. If goals are unrealistically high, you will probably face self-confidence issues. You need to set goals that are only slightly challenging if you have self-confidence issues. You want to go into a match with a mind-set that allows you to breathe freely, not one that ties you up with worry and fear of failure. If someone else, such as a parent or coach, sets unrealistic goals for you, reset them in your performance journal and rely on what you've done in the past and what you are realistically capable of doing in the future as your points of reference. When other people set your goals, they usually base them on what it will take to win or beat another competitor, not on your true capabilities. If you can't confront others to let them know what your goals are for yourself, at least you have them in your performance journal, where the true athlete who you are has a voice.

Positive Self-Talk

Self-talk is the running conversation that goes on in your head nearly 24 hours a day. Even when dreaming you have self-talk. Most of the time you don't really listen to or pay attention to what you are saying, but the words that constantly spin around in your head can have an influence on the images in your mind and your attitude, mood, self-worth, determination, and attention. People may simply be born optimistic or pessimistic, and their self-talk reflects that attitude toward life. But I hope that isn't the case for pessimists, because living constantly in a negative mind-set can't be much fun (or healthy). Athletes excel at beating themselves up through self-talk and negative mind-sets. Sometimes you need negative self-talk to refocus so that you pay attention to the right thing, but self-talk can become destructive and starts to hurt self-confidence if you allow it to continue. Read these two versions of a shooter's self-talk and think about the image or place that you see:

- "I can't believe that last shot was a 7. I have no idea how that happened. What will my coach think? That's really going to hurt my score. I'm letting the team down. I have to shoot three 10s to recover. I hate this. Oh great, my hold is getting worse."

- "OK, that last shot was a 7. I overheld and tried too hard. I'll set the gun down the next time that my hold starts to look like that. The gun didn't stay in the 10 ring after the shot. I'll take the shot as it's going into the center. I'll focus on following through past the shot and mentally staying in the 10 ring. I'll be sharp and ready to react to the perfect hold and sight picture."

These thoughts are common for shooters. One version is destructive, and the other is constructive. In the first version, the shooter is not using information from the past correctly and is worrying about the future (the next three shots). In the second version, the shooter is putting the shot in the past, using what happened as information to readjust the tactics for the next shot plan, and focusing on the present. This shooter is not worried about what others think, what will happen with the next three shots, or what the total score will be. This is an example of putting energy into the things that you can control. Self-talk leads the way for this to happen. How would you rate the level of self-confidence of these two shooters? One has to dig out of a hole mentally and physically. The other doesn't allow a poor shot to shake her or his self-confidence. This shooter knows and believes in a plan for the match and keeps using information in a constructive way to make the next shot better.

Many shooters beat themselves up mentally after a bad shot. The key is to recognize that this is happening, use it as a kick in the pants when needed to get back to working on the right things, and change it up when the self-talk is starting to be destructive. When self-talk is having a negative effect on performance, tell yourself, "Stop it!"; that it's garbage in, garbage out (as the computer programmer saying goes); and that the garbage is ending up on your target.

After you stop the negative or pessimistic self-talk, take stock of the situation. Think about where you are in the match. Think about your match plan and what you should focus on to start making it work or at least improve it. Learn from the past and then close it off. Shut the door on it. Don't let the past carry any weight into your present. Think about what you can accomplish with the shots and time remaining in the match. What kind of shooting will prove to you that you can overcome this challenge? This challenge may come up again, so press on and finish strong, incorporating what you learned into your new plan of action. You always have something to learn and a goal to reach; even with your last shot you can accomplish something. Never give up and never stop trying to improve. Self-talk can lead the way to higher belief in your ability and, ultimately, your self-confidence.

Personal Affirmations

Affirmations are self-talk statements that create an image, thought, or positive mind-set. Affirmations should be realistic and focus on something within your control. Use them to overcome shaky self-confidence.

Here are some examples of a shooter's affirmations:

- "I perform well under match conditions."
- "I love to perform under pressure. It brings out the best in me."
- "I shoot great in the wind. Bring it on."
- "I am mentally inside the 10 ring."
- "I am the 10 shooter."

I used some of these affirmations in the Olympics Games and in the matches leading up to them. They shifted my focus toward challenges that I needed to confront, and they set up the framework through which I would execute my shot plan. Knowing that I had to deal with the wind, for example, I'd think about the wind with a perspective that gave me energy and excitement to separate myself from the rest of the pack. To do that, I had to analyze the wind condition for every shot, exercise patience to adjust my timing to shoot not only when the shot was right but also when the wind was right, and maintain that level of concentration throughout the performance. Affirmations can set up the framework for all of that as long as they deal with the present and carry enough resolve to have a positive effect.

If you are just starting in the sport, using the affirmation "I am an Olympic Champion" probably will not boost your self-confidence for an upcoming match. This kind of unrealistic affirmation is not in the present or under the shooter's control. It represents a challenging long-term goal, but trying to imbed it in your subconscious now will only instill false confidence and not help you learn to use affirmations in a positive way to influence the present. Keep your affirmations focused on the current situation and make them reflect a certain aspect that you know is true. Otherwise, they are just wishful thinking without any resolve. Use affirmations in practice so that they have a positive effect on your mind-set during a match.

Focus Plans

Focus plans are competition strategies that account for the important times before and during competition. They include the key mental and physical variables that you can control to perform your best. Going into a competition, you may have up to four focus plans, depending on the time available and what you are dealing with. We'll look at each of these plans—prematch, prep period, match focus, and refocus—and the period and situation that they cover.

Prematch Plan

The prematch plan deals with the time from the moment that you wake up to the time that you get to the range and set up your gear. After shooting some matches, you will develop your physical and mental approach to competition. You will learn how much time must pass between when you eat and when the match begins and how much you should eat. You want to feel neither too full nor hungry during a match, so find the optimal time to eat so that your body feels right during the match. Not getting enough sleep can negatively affect performance, so learn how much sleep you need. To get sufficient sleep, you must start your prematch plan the night before competition. Know how much time you need between getting up in the morning and feeling awake and ready to shoot. If it's an hour, that's great. Many shooters need more time to get up, shower, eat, stretch, and get their heads together before a match, so they plan accordingly. Some shooters like to perform a little physical activity first thing in the morning to wake up and warm up for the match, so they schedule that activity into their plans.

The prematch plan can account for one to three hours or more. If you shoot in the afternoon and have all day to account for before the match, your plan may last seven or eight hours. The point is to spell out all the physical things that you need to do to feel ready going into the match, as well as the mental aspects of feeling ready and excited to shoot, no matter what time of day the match takes place. Because the start time is out of your control, develop a strategy that has you ready to go, no matter what time you shoot.

This plan won't be as drawn out or extensive as other strategies that you'll develop, but it sets the stage and guarantees that you accomplish everything that you need to do to perform your best and that you are as ready as you can be. Going through your prematch plan consistently will help develop confidence. Because you've done it before, you'll do it again, providing a solid foundation from which to build. The strategy that you'll build on top of the prematch plan is the prep period plan.

Prep Period Plan

Step 7, "Preparing for Competition," introduced beginning elements for a plan. Personalize this plan with both physical and mental elements that you know are critical for your shooting success. This plan may cover only 10, 15, or 20 minutes, depending on how much time you need before and during the preparation period announced by the line officer. Take this time to close off the rest of the world and focus on shooting. The prematch plan takes into account large-ticket items such as waking up, engaging in physical activity, eating, getting to the range with enough time, and organizing your gear, whereas the prep period plan focuses more on mental elements. By this point, your body should be warmed up and ready to go. Shift your attention to your mental needs and follow a routine that gets you focused and sharp for the match.

As you compete, you will learn what you need to do mentally to perform. Many shooters feel tension, excitement, or anxiety just before a match. If those feelings have a negative effect on your performance, develop and follow a strategy that helps you channel that energy into a mind-set that works for you. Use affirmations, reflect on your task goals, think about what it feels like to shoot well, and start saying things to yourself that bring about that feeling or mood. Many shooters listen to music during this time. Music helps them relax and can even create the kind of mood or mind-set that they know they need to perform well. Some shooters use soothing music; others use rock or hip-hop to pump them up. Try various kinds of music in practice to see how they affect your mind-set.

Some shooters use relaxation or imagery techniques during this time to connect with their bodies and load everything into their minds. These mental training techniques will be discussed in more detail later in this step.

Practice imagery and relaxation on the line to mentally focus on the competition to come.

The point is to use this time to your advantage. Instead of looking up and down the line at the competition, have a strategy that uses the time to focus your mind, calm your energy, and channel your thoughts into being productive and ready for the match.

The last minute of this routine is crucial. At this time, look through your sights, take one last dry fire in the prep period, and set that final focus for the whole match. Establish a routine for the last minute of the prep period. Include items to focus on, images to react to, cue words to get you fired up and ready to attack (or relax, as the case may be). Make sure that you are ready to hold nothing back. The strategy for the prep period is unique for each shooter, so figure out what works for you, practice and perfect it in training, and rely on it during the match.

Match Plan

Use the time in the prematch and prep periods wisely so that you are ready and focused to shoot. The match plan is an extension of the previous plans and covers the whole match. This plan focuses on the mental aspects required to perform your best and keeps you in the proper mind-set. As you gain experience, you will get to know your mind and body and recognize the things that help or hurt performance. After you identify characteristics that help performance, be sure to account for them in the match plan. For example, if you know that negative self-talk hurts your performance and motivation, recognize it when it starts and tell yourself to stop. Then get back to imagery or affirmations that re-create the proper mind-set. Keeping the proper match plan for an entire competition is not a sure thing. You will face situations throughout the match that will challenge you to keep focus. By dealing with these situations and putting them in their proper place, you can get back to the plan that allows you to trust yourself and shoot your best.

Overcoming challenging situations may take more than self-talk, imagery, or affirmations. You may need a completely different or specific routine to help you regroup. You need what is known as a refocus plan.

Refocus Plan

One of the exciting things about sport is that you will always have a new challenge to face and deal with as you continue to participate in the game. There are no gimmes or done deals. Sometimes the underdog beats you, and sometimes you beat the underdog. How people deal with challenge or adversity usually determines who performs the best. Legends grow around people who can perform when the going gets tough. You will face new challenges, too. As you continue to progress in the sport, those challenges can define you as a shooter.

Challenges like the following may take you away from your match plan:

- Shooting nine 10s in a row and going for the 100 score

- Shooting three poor shots in a row
- Going for your first record shot after poor sighters
- Breaking your rifle after going for record
- Seeing your target fall off the frame
- Hearing the line officer say that your position isn't legal
- Falling behind on time
- Shooting better than you ever have

Nearly every shooter has faced these challenges. Some shooters are good at recovering from these situations, and others are not. One thing that can help you deal with these situations, or any other surprise, is to have a refocus plan to deal realistically with the situation and recover to get back into your proper mind-set.

Training is the time to develop and practice refocus plans. Don't wait for a match to see how you might handle a challenging situation. When the situation presents itself in training, think about it in a constructive manner and start developing strategies to manage it. If negative talk going on in your head is making the situation worse, tell yourself to stop. Think about what is happening and why. Go to the source of the problem. Is it your hold, attention, timing, or follow-through? Is tension or fatigue creeping in? Are you giving up? These and other questions will help you get to the center of the challenge so that you can start working it out. I call this checking out, taking a moment to check out of shooting for a while and let your mind go in another direction. You can also check out other solutions. Sometimes no matter what you try, nothing seems to help. This is the signal to check out. Let your mind go back to a time when you faced this situation before and think it through again. You may want to get completely off the line, open your journal to match wisdom, and confirm solutions that you've used before. If there aren't any, go back to your strengths and rely on those for the rest of the match. If your timing is off and your hold won't settle down, focus on relaxing as much as you can and excel at following through if that is your strength.

Refocus plans are physical and mental strategies that can get you back into the game quickly and keep you fighting for the last shot. The more situations you face, the more refocus tools you will have to use in the future. Refocus plans help you approach a situation constructively, come up with a plan to correct the issue, and get back into the 10 ring mentally with imagery or focus cue words.

Every shooter is unique; what helps one person regain focus may not work for another. Explore options in various situations, find out what works, and be responsible for using the correct plan. Challenges, especially new ones, can shake self-confidence. Remembering how you dealt with a similar situation and devising a strategy to use during the match can go a long way to stabilizing your self-confidence.

Developing a Mental Blueprint

You develop a mental blueprint of the perfect shot every time you shoot. That blueprint includes your shot plan and mind-set. Mental and physical aspects will come together until they become automatic, eventually to the point that you may not need cue words or self-talk to direct you through the blueprint because they slow you down. Your body and mind will have a path to follow for every shot. You will put down

the gun and reject a shot without even pinpointing the reason. Something in your subconscious will have recognized that a shot element was off, perhaps in the way that you placed the gun to your shoulder or the way that you looked through your sights or your hold. You will not have to put a lot of energy into figuring out the problem; your subconscious does it for you. The key is to trust it.

When something continues to be off, such as tension in your body or consistently incorrect cheek placement, your subconscious will bring it to your attention so that you can deal with it. It's as if you are the CEO of a company. You know what the company produces (10s on the target) and how all the departments work together, but unless you really need to deal with something, it doesn't cross your desk. Other people deal with it automatically until they can't correct the problem. Then you get in there and fix it. This approach saves energy and effort so that you can continue to manage the big picture (your match plan). You deal with the small stuff only when necessary. Trust that experience and a lot of trial and error has honed your blueprint. It doesn't happen overnight or even in one season. That's why it boosts your self-confidence to a high level. Your mental blueprint has been through the toughest aspects of training and competition, and it's the perfect routine that you rely on at your core.

MANAGING STRESS

Self-confidence and stress are closely related. The lower your self-confidence is in a situation, the higher your stress is. A high level of stress has a negative physical effect. It increases heart rate, blood pressure, sweating, muscle tension, and adrenalin. Mentally, high stress causes feelings of being overwhelmed, narrow attention, confusion, inability to concentrate, and high levels of worry and doubt.

Nearly all athletes feel stress. The successful ones learn to reduce their stress to a controllable range or prevent the situation from creating high stress by keeping the match in perspective and setting realistic and achievable goals.

Goals are also related to stress. If you set task goals that you control and realistic performance goals, stress will feel more like excitement and positive challenge. If your outcome goals are not within your control or your score goals are unrealistic, stress will reach the anxiety range and hurt your self-confidence and performance. Stress can be positive if goals are in line and push your ability, not stomp on it.

The first key to managing stress is to manage your goals. Make sure that goals push you enough to be challenging and exciting to reach. If they are too high or based on someone else's performance, you will waste energy focusing on elements outside your control. If you worry about what someone else will do in the competition, you waste energy on worry and doubt for no reason. Put the energy into your performance and the tasks that you control.

The next factor is to identify the level of stress at which you perform your best. Judge your stress level on a scale of 1 to 10. At 10, the highest level, you feel anxiety that leads to a poor performance. Level 5 is right in the middle. At this level, you feel excitement and positive expectation and have a good performance. Level 1 is associated with feelings of boredom and being completely unchallenged.

You would think that shooters would want to feel something in the range of 2 to 5 to perform free of stress. After all, they would be relaxed, with no doubt or worry affecting them. This circumstance may be true for some shooters. Others want to feel a little pressure. They use stress to sharpen their instincts and increase their drive to perform their best. I used to feel around a 7 or 8 when I performed my best. That level wasn't relaxing or even comfortable, but it gave me the feeling that I needed to be sharp and focused for the competition. That level of stress didn't have a negative effect on my body, but it might have on someone else.

After you identify the stress level at which you perform your best, work on getting to and maintaining that level throughout the match. A couple of tools that you can use to increase or decrease feelings and effects of stress are relaxation and imagery.

Relaxation

Use relaxation to lower the feelings of stress or tension in your body. We'll quickly cover some of the many relaxation techniques so that you'll know how to find out more about them, and we'll go into depth with one so that you can start to work with it right away.

The environment for learning relaxation is similar for all these techniques. Find a quiet place where you won't be disturbed. Lie on your back or recline in a chair and dim the lights if you can. This is better than having a bright or completely dark room. Play soothing music or nature sounds, if you wish. Use slow deep breaths to connect your body physically to relaxation. Focus on your exhalations. Release physical and mental tension with each exhalation.

Progressive Relaxation

Progressive relaxation involves tensing and relaxing specific muscles or groups of muscles at a time and then focusing on the feeling of relaxation that goes along with the release of the tension. For example, clench your fists tight. Think about the tension running up your forearms and into your biceps. Try to develop as much tension as possible for about five seconds. Then take a deep breath, and with a slow exhalation, use a cue phrase or word such as "let it go" or "relax" or "drift" as you unclench your fists and let the tension drain away from the muscles in your arms and hands. Take another deep breath, use the cue phrase or word again, and try to feel even deeper levels of relaxation in your arms and hands as the tension drains away.

Begin by lying on your back. Start with your head and face and work in groups all the way down your body to your toes. Include your face and jaw in one tensing; your neck and shoulders in the next; your fists, forearms, and biceps in the next; your abdominals in the next; your gluteal muscles and hamstrings in the next; and your feet and calves for the finish. The key is to tie together the breathing, cue phrase or word, and the release of tension and then to feel in control of the whole effort.

When you get to the range to shoot, you may do progressive relaxation as part of your pre-match plan, but it is too extensive to use in the middle of the match. That's where the breathing and cue words come into play. Use them to focus on the tension in your body. Because of the relaxation training that you've done, your body will respond to the "let it go" cue by releasing stress and tension. Doing this takes practice. Although you won't feel the levels of stress and tension in training that you do in a match, you need to make these responses work during practice if you ever want them to work in a match.

Biofeedback

If other relaxation techniques are not having any effect, try biofeedback. Biofeedback machines are becoming more user friendly and cost effective, so you may be able to find one locally. A biofeedback machine usually has a simple attachment, called a galvanic skin response device, that you lay your fingers on. Some have devices that can be attached to tense areas, such as the shoulders or back. The device picks up changes in your heart rate, skin temperature, or muscle activity. When tension is perceived, the machine makes a constant clicking noise. As you relax and reduce the tension in your body, the noise level of the machine diminishes. Your goal is to reduce the noise level to as low as possible.

This type of training mainly increases awareness of tension in the body and lets you try relaxation techniques to alleviate it. The machine is useful for monitoring your body as you imagine stressful situations. Learn what those situations do to your body and use your refocus plans to get back under physical control.

Imagery Relaxation

This technique uses two mental training tools at once. The first is a simple form of imagery, and the second is the relaxation response. Simply close your eyes and think of a place where you felt relaxed and secure. You may find yourself on a beach listening to the waves, taking a walk in the forest, or sitting in your grandparents' backyard. You can even make up a place that provides a quiet, peaceful, and relaxed atmosphere. Your goal is to become as relaxed as possible throughout your whole body while imagining yourself in this special place. Focus on feeling yourself there. Hear the sounds associated with the location, feel the sun on your face, smell the scents that come along. Involve as many of your senses as possible to immerse yourself into the location.

The key to this relaxation technique is to have your body respond when you bring up the image. Then you can start to use it in situations of high stress and feel the same bodily response to regain some control. Instead of using cue words and deep breaths to bring about the relaxation response as in progressive relaxation training, imagery relaxation uses picture and deep breathing to bring about the response. Try both to see whether one works better for you than the other or try a combination of both techniques.

Self-Directed Relaxation

This technique is similar to progressive relaxation because it focuses on specific muscle groups one at a time. The difference is that you perform no physical tensing and relaxing of the muscle. Instead, you focus on a specific muscle or muscle group and simply think about or imagine the tension draining away from your body. Use slow, deep breaths. With each exhalation, use a cue word to direct the tension out of your body.

You are more likely to use this technique on the shooting range than you do other techniques because it's fast and specific to a particular body part, such as your shoulders or back. The key is to practice and practice some more. Self-directed relaxation won't work like magic in a match if you try it then for the first time. You must develop a strong connection between your breathing, cue word, and muscle response, and doing that requires training.

Self-directed relaxation is wonderful because you can quickly become proficient at it with training. The response time becomes shorter as you use it more.

Try this self-directed relaxation script. Have someone read it to you slowly with the accompaniment of relaxing music or record it with music and use it with headphones anywhere you choose. I'll use the phrase "Let it go" as the relaxation cue words in the script. If you want to use another cue, just insert it where you see that phrase and you're ready to go.

"Close your eyes and focus on your breathing. Breathe in slowly through your nose to the count of four and out through your mouth to the count of four. Think about filling your lungs from the bottom up, bringing in the air so deeply that your abdomen rises, not your chest. Bring in more and more fresh air to fill your lungs and refresh your whole body. With each slow exhalation, think 'Let it go.' Connect your breathing with all the tension leaving your body. Take three more slow, controlled breaths and think 'Let it go' as you slowly exhale through your mouth.

"Shift your focus to your face. Inhale slowly. As you exhale, think about the tension in your forehead, cheeks, and jaw draining away. It's leaving your face and draining into the floor, leaving your body forever. Slowly inhale and think 'Let it go,' as even more tension drains away from your face and head. Your face feels relaxed, the muscles feel heavy, and your jaw is limp. Take one more deep breath, let it go, and your face is totally relaxed.

"Moving into your neck and shoulders now, think about breathing cool air deep into your lungs. As the air flows back out, tension is carried away from your neck and shoulders and out of your body. With each breath in and out, let it go. Tension is leaving your body forever. Your shoulders feel relaxed and limp. Feel gravity bring them to the ground as all the tension drains completely away. Take one more slow breath. As you exhale, focus on your neck and shoulders as they relax even more and sink deeper into feeling heaviness.

"Now focus on your arms. As you inhale, think about the tension in your arms. As you exhale, the breath pushes the tension from your shoulders down your arms to your hands and out the ends of your fingertips. Each breath helps to let it go. Each wave releases more and more tension, to be pushed out of your body forever. Your arms feel limp, warm, and heavy. Each exhalation makes them more and more relaxed as you let it go. Your arms feel so relaxed that they are almost floating. Let it go, let all the tension drain away.

"Focus on your chest and abdomen. Imagine a centerline from your neck to your belly button. As you inhale, the line turns warm and rises with your breath. As you exhale, the line splits in half down the center and carries all the tension in your chest and abdomen with it to the sides of your body and down into the floor. Each breath carries a wave of relaxation across

your chest and abdomen and drains away the tension through your back and into the floor. Let it go. Your chest feels relaxed, your abdomen feels warm, and your back feels heavy. Breathe through these areas a few more times and relax even deeper.

"Thinking about your hips now, use the same line that splits across your hips and carries a wave of relaxation over your hip bones, down through your gluteal muscles, and into the floor. With each breath in and out, let it go. Your muscles are feeling more and more relaxed, the tension continues to drain away, and the warm wave of your breath is carrying any last lingering amount of stress away with it.

"Focusing on your legs, use the same wave of relaxation that you used with your arms. As you inhale, imagine a wave forming at the top of your hip. As you exhale, the wave moves down your leg to your foot and drains into the floor at your heel. The wave carries any tension from your quads, hamstrings, and calves, and lets it go right into the floor at your heel. Any tension in your foot also drains back to the heel and leaves your body forever. Take some more deep breaths. As each wave goes down your leg, your leg becomes heavier, warmer, and completely limp. Let it go, let all the tension drain away.

"Now that your entire body has been completely released of stress and tension, do a couple of body waves. Take a slow, deep breath and imagine a warm wave moving down your body from your face to your feet, carrying with it any last amounts of tension from your body. With each breath, each wave increases the feelings of relaxation. Your body feels so relieved that it's almost floating above the floor. Connect with that feeling. Realize that you can create it whenever you want to. You are in control of your body by letting the tension go. Take a few more deep breaths and enjoy this feeling of peacefulness and calm for your body and mind."

The first few times that you go through a relaxation session, you may find your mind wandering, be unable to connect to the right area of the body, or have trouble letting go of tension. This new form of training has such a connection with the mind that you may need a few sessions before your thoughts, breaths, and muscles are in harmony. Practice will make it easier. You will be able to relax by using your cue words, focusing on the troubled area in your body, and breathing out the tension. If nothing else, relaxation connects your breath and body so that you start to feel at least some control. When under high stress, use this as the first defense so that you can complete the rest of your match plan or refocus plan.

Imagery

Imagery can be a powerful mental training tool if you direct it toward your specific needs. It can be part of your focus plans, your relaxation cue, your shot blueprint, and your mind-set. Imagery ties together as many senses as possible to create the perfect mental performance. Create the physical feeling that you need to shoot a good shot and combine it with what you want to see and what you want to happen. Bring in any other senses, such as hearing or smell, to the image to increase the intensity. The one place where you can perform perfectly, any time you want to, is in your mind. The more often you mentally rehearse and immerse yourself in a perfect performance, the more likely you are to believe that you are capable of achieving it. You will start to trust yourself in and out of stressful situations.

As with relaxation training, imagery takes time to develop and perfect. Start simply by imagining a perfect sight picture. If you have trouble doing this, look back at figure 5.5 (page 62) and then close your eyes and try to see that sight picture in your head. This is what you want to see when you take a shot. This should be the last thought that you have before you actually shoot. If you load this image into your head before you shoot, you are ready to react when you see it happen. You'll probably also reject shots that aren't lining up correctly because they aren't matching the criteria that you require.

This type of imagery (as if you are actually looking with your eyes) is called internal imag-ery. Some athletes use external imagery, which is seeing images as if you are watching yourself on video. The athlete sees him- or herself perfectly performing a skill, such as a tennis serve, a free throw, or golf shot. Because shooters don't have any movement to perfect, only the movement in the hold and timing, stick with internal imagery. Then you can focus on the meat of the matter—what a perfect shot looks and feels like and how it responds.

After you can control creating and holding a perfect sight picture in your head, add additional variables. Add movement to the sight picture, such as what you would see in a normal hold. Add timing your shot through that movement as the hold settles down over the 10 ring. Do it in slow motion at first and work up to regular speed. After you master that, put yourself in different situations and imagine taking solid shots no matter what challenge you face.

Here are a few situations that may challenge you, and ways to imagine yourself through them realistically:

• Imagine yourself taking your first shot for record perfectly. Back up in time and take your last two sighting shots. Feel confident from them. Adjust your position to your first record bull and shoot a perfect first shot. You can shoot your first record shot in imagery hundreds of times; getting that much specific training in practice is difficult. This example shows that you can pinpoint a challenge and rehearse, rehearse, rehearse. Perfectly, of course.

• Imagine yourself behind on time at the end of a match with three shots to go. Think about the stress of the situation. Use your relaxation cues and go to work in imagery to shoot three more perfect shots under control. Focus on your blueprint and trust your hold and timing. Remember to follow through.

• Imagine yourself at the regional championships. The shooters around you are outstanding, but you have come to shoot your own match plan, achieve your own task goals, and earn a score that means something to you. Although this is a new situation, you rely on your strengths, which keep you focused on what you can control. You feel excitement, not anxiety.

• Imagine yourself in a final. In your head, hear the line officer say, "For your first round, load. Attention, 3, 2, 1. Start." Imagine the perfect shot. Hear the line officer call out your score for everyone to hear: "Shooter number one, 10.7." Imagine yourself a point ahead of the pack, or a point behind, and then shooting a perfect shot. Imagine the last shot of the final (use different challenging situations) and shoot a perfect shot.

• Imagine yourself shooting a perfect shot after realizing that you're shooting better than you ever have before.

• Imagine yourself shooting a perfect shot after having a bad string. You don't have to think about shooting the bad shots; just pretend that they are on your target and that you need to recover. Constructively think about what you want

to do to get your hold under control, sharpen your timing, and create a follow-through that stays right over the 10 ring. Imagine the perfect shot after dealing with the physical aspects that you're going to change.

• Imagine the last shot of the match. You can be shooting well, or perhaps you need this last shot to be in your score range. Put the pressure on yourself in imagery. Decide how to handle the challenge constructively and perform the perfect shot.

Everyone approaches challenges differently. A situation that is distressing for one person may fuel the success of another. On your shooting journey, you will face various situations that will challenge or stress you. Learn imagery and relaxation skills to help you mentally and physically deal with these challenges as they arise. You will be well on your way to being a consistent and successful performer in all that you do.

TRAINING PHYSICALLY

Many people think that because shooters stand still, physical training has no effect on performance. The truth is that the top shooters in the world are extremely fit and rely heavily on physical training to build endurance, body control, flexibility, and strength and to relieve stress. Check with your doctor before starting any physical training program.

Endurance Training

Endurance is built through aerobic exercise, which trains the heart to increase its size, strength, and efficiency. Aerobic exercise also trains the lungs and blood vessels to deliver adequate amounts of oxygen to cells to meet the demands of prolonged physical activity.

Aerobic exercise is any physical activity that can be done over a period of time to increase demand on the heart, which raises the heart rate into a training target zone. Your age and level of fitness determine the heart rate that defines this range. The training target zone is a guideline that lets you know whether the exercise intensity is

too hard, too easy, or just right to increase the efficiency of your aerobic system.

Training to increase endurance includes jogging, biking, cross-country skiing, swimming, inline skating, aerobics classes, or any other physical activity that increases your heart rate into your training zone and that you can do for 20 minutes or longer. Your doctor may recommend that you start with 15 minutes and build up to a longer period. Your goal should be to do the activity for 20 to 40 minutes or longer, depending on your level of fitness and desired training goal. If you want to maintain your level of fitness, exercising every other day is sufficient. If you want to improve your level of fitness, exercise four to six days each week.

Strength Training

Strength training builds muscle fibers and can help prevent injury, improve coordination, and increase body control. If your doctor hasn't given you a specific exercise prescription, design a program that works all areas of your body for overall balance and stability. Unlike endurance training, strength training should not be done daily. Muscles need about 48 hours to recover from a training session. They need that interval to build muscle fibers. Many strength-training programs are available. Choose one that fits your goals and is convenient for you. Two good books to consult if you are new to strength training are *Weight Training: Steps to Success, Third Edition*, by Thomas Baechle and Roger Earle (2006, Human Kinetics), and *Weight Training Fundamentals* by David Sandler (2003, Human Kinetics).

Weight Training

If you have access to a weight room or a fitness club, weight training is probably the easiest and fastest way to build a strength-training routine. Weight machines are convenient, and a professional at a fitness club can help you perform lifts correctly and develop a program to improve your overall physical strength. In general, you want to work all the major muscle groups of the body. If you can go every day, focus on the upper body one day and the lower body the next. Work up to three sets of lifts and 8 to 12 repetitions per set. If you can't get to 8 repetitions, you are tearing down too much muscle and will be really sore. If you're able to go higher than 12 repetitions, you are not stressing the muscle enough to create significant strength gains. These guidelines will help you get started. Talk with your doctor or a trainer for additional information about developing a weightlifting program to fit your needs.

Strength Training Without Weights

You can also gain strength without using a weight room. Using only the space in your home and a few handy pieces of equipment, you can do push-ups, sit-ups, pull-ups, lunges, squats, chair dips, step-ups, and arm curls. The intensity may not be as high as what you can achieve with weights, but by using your body weight for resistance, you can improve your overall strength with consistent workout routines.

Core Training

Core strength is important in shooting because we use core muscles to stabilize the standing and kneeling positions. Although we try to relax as much as possible, we still engage the core, especially in standing position. Core exercises work the abdomen and back, and can go down into the hips as well. Holding exercises coordinate balance and stability. Core exercises include the plank, the star, feet to ball, inchworm, and ball stand. Many books and other instructional material on building core strength are available. Examine a few and do a variety of exercises for fun and a well-rounded strength routine.

Martial Arts and Yoga

If you participate in a martial art such as tai chi, karate, or kung-fu, you are well on your way to developing a philosophy of using your mind and body to work together to gain strength, coordination, and self-control. The discipline taught through the martial arts will help you develop patience, gather strength, and control your body to perform challenging tasks perfectly. The fitness that comes along with martial arts training is a bonus because it increases core strength, endurance, and muscular strength. If you are looking for an enjoyable activity that pushes the norms of being an everyday shooter, look into the martial arts or yoga classes offered in your area and add one to your physical and mental fitness regimen.

SUCCESS SUMMARY OF TRAINING MENTALLY AND PHYSICALLY

By finishing this step, you have gained a clear understanding about how goals can help you manage your focus, self-confidence, motivation, and stress. Many of these mental factors are linked together. Learn to use each one to your advantage depending on the situation and challenge that you face. Learning to turn destructive behavior into constructive aids will serve you well on your performance journey.

Focus plans are an important part of any serious athlete's training and competition regimen. Work to identify the important factors that go into a good performance and be responsible for accounting for each one. Have a focus plan to use before the match, during preparation, while sighting in, when going for record, and during the match, and have a plan to recover or refocus when obstacles or opportunities come your way.

Top shooters are physically fit. Adding a fitness program to your schedule not only helps your shooting but also supports good health in your life as a whole.

The next step covers organizations that support three-position air rifle programs and shooting camps. You will learn what to expect when looking into collegiate shooting. All these experiences can lead you to the national team or national development team. If you stick with the sport, you may well have the chance to make it on to the team that represents your country in international competition. That is a reward in itself and an exciting long-term goal to work toward.

Before Taking the Next Step

Before moving on to step 11, Continuing in the Sport, evaluate what you have learned to this point. Answer each of the following questions honestly. If you can answer all seven questions, you are ready to move on to the next step.

1. Have you set long-term and short-term goals for this shooting season?
2. Have you set up matches along the way as benchmarks to work toward and to help determine your current ability level?
3. Have you thought about your self-confidence and stress levels going into a match as well as in practice?
4. Have goal setting, self-talk, affirmations, and imagery had an effect on your self-confidence and stress levels?
5. Have you tried relaxation training?
6. Have you incorporated a relaxation cue word into your shot plan to help you check your body before you pick up the rifle?
7. Have you incorporated a physical fitness program into your overall training plan?

Continuing in the Sport

Shooting is a sport that anyone can participate in. With hard work and dedication, you can achieve the highest levels or you can continue to shoot in your area and enjoy local matches. Whether you are a competitive person or one who just likes to try to better your last best score, shooting can teach you a lot about perseverance, mental toughness, and being your best when it counts.

"START!"

Now is the time to get going in the sport. Many resources can help you find programs, teams, and organizations in your area that offer three-position air rifle and other shooting opportunities. Start by calling all the shooting ranges in your area to see whether they support a junior program or have a junior team. Look on the Internet for the rifle and pistol association for your state. Some cities or counties have rifle and pistol associations, so search for those as well. When you contact your local organizations, ask about the shooting sports in your area, particularly junior teams and air rifle opportunities.

Here is a list of national organizations that can help you. Contact information is available in Additional Resources. You may have to use a search engine to find organizations that have changed Web addresses.

- The American Legion is the world's largest wartime veterans organization. It supports many youth programs including scouting, baseball, boy's nation and boy's state, oratorical, and junior shooting sports.

- The Civilian Marksmanship Program (CMP) network of affiliated shooting clubs and associations cover every state in the United States. Through their network of clubs and associations, all qualified U.S. citizens may receive firearms safety training and marksmanship courses as well as the opportunity for continued practice and competition.

- The National 4-H Shooting Sports Program focuses on developing youth as individuals and as responsible and productive citizens by encouraging marksmanship, the safe and responsible use of firearms, the principles of hunting and archery, and more. Youth receive opportunities to develop life skills, self-worth, and conservation ethics.

- Army, Marine Corps, and Navy JROTC programs may offer opportunities for shooting. Check your high school or the CMP Web site.

- USA Shooting is the national governing body for the sport of shooting, as chartered by the U.S. Olympic Committee. USA Shooting implements and manages development programs and sanctions events at the local, state, regional, and national levels.

- The National Rifle Association provides a list of matches and coming events in each state. If you want to try other shooting disciplines, this is a good place to start.

- The National Three-Position Air Rifle Council includes the American Legion, BSA-Venturing, CMP, Daisy/U.S. Jaycees Shooter Education Program, National 4-H Shooting Sports, the U.S. Army Marksmanship Unit, USA Shooting, and the Army, Marine Corps, and Navy JROTC commands.

FINDING MATCHES

In the best-case scenario, you will have many teams and matches in your area from which to choose. If you do, select the program that fits your needs and provides the opportunities that you want to have as you progress in the sport. If you want only to practice and shoot on your own, join the local gun club and shoot at your own pace when the desire strikes. If you want to compete and shoot in local matches, look into the club teams and their competition schedules. These programs can be an excellent place to start to focus on local competitions. Local competitions can lead to state championships and even regional championships. Find listings in shooting publications, on the Web site of a club, or on the Web site of your state rifle and pistol association. Most ranges host some type of annual match, so you may discover an active network of shooters and competitions.

If you want to shoot in larger competitions and possibly travel to shoot in national championships, programs such as the American Legion, JROTC, and local clubs that vie for spots at the NRA National Team Air-Rifle Championships are worth looking into. Another exciting competition is the National Junior Olympic Three-Position Air Rifle Championships. You can find contact information in Additional Resources.

One of the best junior championships to qualify for is the Junior Olympic National Championships (JORC). This tournament is held every year at the Olympic Training Center in Colorado Springs, Colorado. Each state has a qualifying match for this event. If you win the qualifying match or shoot a qualifying score at the state level, you will be invited to participate at the JORC. All the best juniors in the country are at this match; participating in this event is an excellent goal to set. The events shot are the same as the Olympic events: a 60-shot air rifle match (all standing) for men and a 40-shot air rifle match (all standing) for women. Small-bore matches are also held. Unless you are training and competing in small bore, focus on the air rifle event. Go to the USA Shooting Web site and look under Competitions to find out where in your state the qualifiers will be held. You can even go to another state if necessary to shoot the qualifiers. You won't be able to win the slot for that state's representative, which is an automatic invite, but you can still be invited if you shoot a qualifying score. These scores may change, so you should look them up on the USA Shooting Web site.

Winners at the JORC earn a USA Shooting Team jacket. This coveted jacket means that you have earned a slot on the U.S. national development team by winning the national championship. If you work hard, someday you can be up there too.

ATTENDING SHOOTING CAMPS

As you work up to shooting at higher levels, you can benefit by being on a team that can help you get where you want to go in the sport. Having other shooters around for support and a coach to learn from is helpful, but it's not essential. If a team isn't available, you can train and shoot on your own, enter matches individually, and compete with everyone else.

If you are training on your own, look into summer camps for some coaching and a chance to meet other shooters. At a shooting camp, you will get an intense week of instruction from knowledgeable coaches who will examine your positions inside and out and give useful advice on what you need to work on.

The CMP offers one-week camps all over the country. The NRA also has summer camps to fit various levels of ability. You can find their contact information in Additional Resources.

Individual coaches or schools may offer camps that last a weekend or three days. These specialty camps may be advertised in shooting sports magazines from the NRA or USA Shooting, or in publications of other shooting organizations.

If because of your age you no longer qualify as a junior or are ineligible to join an organized youth program, participate at your local shooting range with the senior clubs. Senior clubs usually focus on a particular discipline such as bench rest, silhouette, or prone shooting, but this may open the door to a variety of new disciplines and ways to enjoy the sport. If you want to pursue making the national team, find a range where you can practice the international disciplines and attend matches sanctioned by USA Shooting. That way you can get some quality international-style experience and work toward attending USA Shooting's National Championship, which is held every summer. The national coach uses this match to select shooters for the U.S. national and development teams for the upcoming year. At this time, only junior shooters can qualify for the development team. You must be one of the top three shooters at the championships to qualify for the national team.

As you can see, multiple opportunities are available to you to get out there and start competing. A national champion may be shooting right beside you at one of these matches. In this sport, you will rub elbows with some of the best in the country, even at your local ranges. Competition is competition. Whether it's a local match, a sectional, a tryout, or a national championship, shooters are out there perfecting their game and gaining experience through whatever venue provides an opportunity. After you get involved in the game, you'll soon see where all the opportunities are for you to participate and succeed.

SHOOTING ON THE COLLEGIATE LEVEL

The options listed for clubs, camps, and organizations focus on the junior high (or middle school) to high school years. You may meet junior shooters from other states and form lasting friendships. You may meet up with them again and become teammates at the college level. Slightly fewer than 40 colleges offer rifle as an NCAA varsity sport. Scholarships are available, and participants have a chance to shoot all over the country in NCAA competition. NCAA shooters compete to represent their universities at the NCAA National Rifle Championship. The college courses of fire are 60 shots standing for air rifle and a 3 × 20 in small bore. Four-person teams compete in each event. Scores are added together for a team total. Most shooters shoot both events, so you don't have to specialize in just one gun.

This book focuses on three-position air rifle, but the foundation built through this discipline will cross over into three-position small bore. The position elements are the same. Small bore features more supportive equipment, such as a butt hook, palm rest, and an abundance of butt plate and cheek piece adjustments to fit your body. You should learn to shoot without all the extra equipment used in small bore because your body and mind learn to shoot through challenge and position refinement. When starting out on advanced small-bore rifles with myriad adjustments to make, many shooters become caught up in changing their equipment whenever they face a challenge and don't ever really learn to shoot.

Competing on a varsity team at the college level is exciting and challenging. You will be able to practice daily, a change for many junior shooters who trained only two or three days a week before college. Training every day may seem excessive, but after you go up against other schools, you'll see that it takes that much training to keep up with the competition. Varsity collegiate shooting is not for the average weekend shooter. You need to have motivation, drive, and determination to succeed on this stage. Varsity teams are allowed to train 20 hours a week, and they must fit range training, physical training, mental training, and meetings into that block of time. Accomplishing everything that needs to be done during the week is challenging.

Look for the NRA in Additional Resources to find information about how to contact colleges.

Because rifle is sponsored by the NCAA, college coaches, recruits, and student-athletes must follow recruiting rules. Because that rule book is extremely thick and the rules change year by year, we'll focus on what you can do to get started. You are allowed to contact coaches by phone or e-mail at any time. You can send them your resume and let them know that you are interested in their programs. Fill out the team questionnaire, if they have one, and ask questions about the university and its majors. You can visit universities as many times as you want to, at your own expense, to get a feel for the place, team, and coach. These visits are called unofficial visits.

College coaches can start actively recruiting you when you are a high school senior. They can call you once a week and bring you to the university on what is called an official visit. For this 48-hour tour of the facilities, the school pays for your trip. Before you can go on an official visit, you must register with the NCAA Eligibility Center. This certification done by the NCAA will confirm that you are academically eligible to compete at the college division I, II, and III levels. Your file won't be complete until your high school sends your final grades, but the process must be started before you're allowed to go on official visits. Start looking into this when you are a junior if possible. You can find NCAA contact information in Additional Resources.

During this exciting time in your life you can visit up to five universities on official visits as you decide where you want to go with your shooting and academic future. To get ready to introduce yourself to the coaches at the universities that you are interested in, put together a shooting resume to show your progress in the sport and your interest in joining their teams.

For your shooting resume, include this personal information:

- Name, address, home phone number, cell phone number, e-mail address
- Graduation year, grade point average, test scores
- High school information, counselor's name
- Possible majors
- Shooting club or organization information, shooting coach's information

You also need to provide shooting information:

- Length of your experience in an organized program
- Frequency (per week) and location of your practice sessions
- Events that you shoot
- Rifles and gear that you own
- Your shooting goals

List the matches that you've participated in for the past two or three years if you have been shooting that long. Include the date, location, and name of the match, your scores, and the place that you finished. The most important information is your scores. In addition, list any camps that you've attended and any other sports that you participate in.

When coaches see this information, they will recognize that you are serious about the sport and want to go to a team and coach who will help you reach your goals. They may want additional information, but this initial information lets them know that you have your act together.

Competing on a varsity team may be more than you want to do in college. The time commit-ment and frequent travel make it a focus point for a shooter's entire college experience. If that sort of commitment is too much for you but you'd still like to do some shooting at the college level, you may want to consider the shooting clubs offered at many universities. In these more low-key programs, participants shoot perhaps a couple of days a week, compete a few times a year, and don't have to follow the rigorous NCAA rules to be in a sport. More information on finding university and ROTC shooting clubs is listed in Additional Resources.

APPLYING TO MILITARY ACADEMIES

Nearly all the military academies have a varsity rifle team. Attending a military academy is a big decision and commitment on your part, so take time to research the opportunity to decide whether you want to pursue this avenue. Many of the academies offer full scholarships that include an exceptional education and the chance to shoot against other NCAA varsity teams. In most cases, graduates are required to complete five years of service after graduation, so you need to decide whether this choice is right for you.

The recruiting process is different from that of other colleges and universities. Coaches from military academies can start calling prospects once a week during their junior year of high school. This procedure helps you through the admissions process, which is more extensive than that used to apply to a standard state or private university. If you are interested in going to a military academy, get started. You will need to devote a lot of time during your junior and senior years to completing all the forms, interviews, the physical, and the fitness test. If you are already in the last semester of your senior year, it's probably too late. But it never hurts to see whether you can still finish the process. Go to the institution's admissions Web site and go for it.

COMPETING IN SMALL-BORE RIFLE AND ON NATIONAL TEAMS

In a collegiate program, unless it's an air rifle only team, you'll be introduced to and eventually compete in small-bore rifle. This is the next step of growth in the sport. You may have a junior team in your area that sponsors this discipline as well as air rifle. If so, take advantage of it when you're ready to take on a new challenge.

Small bore provides more opportunities to compete at the college level, and it's another event that offers you an opportunity to join the U.S. national development team (NDT). At certain matches during a shooting season, shooters can earn places on the NDT. Currently, the individual winners of the NCAA Championships, the shooter with the highest collegiate match average, the winner of the National JORC, and the top performers at the USA Shooting National Championships are selected for the NDT. To determine what matches are used for the coming year, check the USA Shooting Team Web site or contact the national rifle team coach.

The top three shooters in each Olympic event at USA Shooting's National Championships are selected for the U.S. national team. Juniors can qualify to be on the national team if they place in the top three overall at the nationals. This team will have first choice on trips to World Cups and other important matches because they are the strongest contenders to earn a place on the next Olympic team.

In international small-bore events, women shoot a 3 × 20. Men shoot a 3 × 40 and a 60-shot prone match. The women have a 60-shot prone match in the world championships but not in the Olympic Games. Small bore is shot outdoors at 50 meters in international competition, which adds to focus plans the challenge of changing wind, lighting, and weather.

The main international match for the U.S. team rotates through a four-year cycle. The first match in the cycle is the Championship of Americas, open only to shooters from countries in North, Central, and South America. The next year is the World Shooting Championships; all countries are invited. The third year in the rotation features the Pan American Games. This event is open to the countries that shoot in the Championship of Americas, and it replicates the Olympic Games by having events in all sports. You live in an athlete's village, walk in an opening ceremony, and compete just as you would in the Olympic Games. The fourth year is the match that all the others are used to prepare for—the Olympic Games.

The Olympics can become the pinnacle of your journey. Not every sport that starts in a basement or living room (doing holding exercises) can take you all the way to the Olympic Games, but this one can. Just imagine. You start out with an air rifle or sporter rifle aiming at a dot on the wall in your bedroom and end up on an Olympic awards stand, representing your country, your team, and your family. You can't have a better feeling in the world. The journey can be long and challenging, and you will face setbacks. But it will also teach you to believe in yourself, work for what counts, and be the best that you can be when it matters most. Only a few make it to the Olympic Games, but those who do have a strong sense of direction, immense motivation, and a drive that just won't permit them to give up when the going gets tough. If you are or want to be a person like this, get on board.

SUCCESS SUMMARY OF CONTINUING IN THE SPORT

This step has exposed you to a variety of organizations and resources that will help you find opportunities to begin and continue your shooting journey. The local level includes youth organizations, JROTC teams, shooting clubs at local ranges, and junior teams. At the national level, you can look to the NRA, USA Shooting, the National Three-Position Air Rifle Council, and the CMP for help finding matches, clubs, teams, and camps around the country.

If you are looking to shoot in college, start to build a shooter's resume and research the universities or military academies of your choice to see whether they are a fit to your academic, shooting, and career goals. Contact those coaches if they haven't contacted you and let them know that you are interested in their programs. Collegiate competition offers the opportunity to travel around the country to other universities and possibly make the U.S. national development team if you have the highest average or win the NCAA National Championships.

Being on the NT or NDT opens a door to the world. You will have the chance to train at high-level training camps and represent the United States in international competition. With dedication and a willingness to stay in the sport for the long haul, you could make it all the way to the world championships or Olympic Games. Those opportunities don't come to shooters who are looking to be overnight sensations. They come to the shooters who have tried and failed, kept working when others gave up, and never let go of the belief that they had something special inside. Through adversity comes strength, and those are the qualities that you'll see in shooters on the national team.

Congratulations on climbing the steps to success in three-position air rifle shooting. You have selected the right equipment and rifle for your size and shape, you know how to be safe around rifles and ranges, you know how to set up your rifle to fit your body, and you have established your positions and trained them for consistency. You are keeping track of changes to your rifle, positions, and accomplishments in your shooter's journal. That information will help you conserve time and energy in the future when you face similar challenges and opportunities.

As you move into competition, you are ready to face a variety of conditions at different ranges and events. You are ready to roll with the punches on your road of experience. You have gained mental toughness and learned to manage challenging matches and finals. With the support of proper goal setting, you have high self-confidence and are able to manage stress because you have the right mind-set. Use relaxation, imagery, self-talk, affirmations, and your perfect shot blueprint to help manage the task at hand. All these tools will serve you well as you grow in the sport and take on larger and more demanding challenges. Enjoy the journey. You can apply the lessons that you learn in shooting to many areas of your life. Reach your full potential through the long-term goals that inspire you most.

■⌐ Glossary

9 ring—First ring around the 10 on the target; a shot that touches or breaks this ring scores 9 points.

10 ring (also called the 10 or center)—Dot in the center of the target; a shot that touches or takes out all or part of the 10 ring scores 10 points.

40-shot standing—Course of fire used for women's international air rifle events.

60-shot standing—Course of fire used for men's international air rifle events.

action—The air cylinder, regulator, and operating system that closes over a pellet so that the air rifle can shoot.

air cylinder—Small compressed-air tube that screws into the regulator.

air rifle—Rifle that uses compressed air or CO_2 gas to propel a pellet.

anticipate the shot—Timing to take the shot as the hold is moving into the 10 ring instead of moving out of it.

aperture—Circle of metal, glass, or plastic that is inserted into the front sight and that has a small black open ring in the center that is used to center the rifle on the bull. The black ring in the center comes in different sizes. Shooters use a size based on how big their hold is. A larger hold means using a larger aperture.

backer target—Empty target placed a couple of inches (centimeters) behind a record target to show the direction that a pellet came from if it was cross-fired from another shooter. Backer targets are required at some matches but not all. Target holders are designed to hold the backer behind the record target.

barrel—Steel tube with rifling on the rifle that the pellet is shot through.

bipod—Small two-pronged armature attached under the front of the stock when the rifle is not in use to keep it upright when it is resting on the ground.

blinder—Small piece of plastic or paper that shooters use to cover the nonaiming eye.

breech—Area at the back of the barrel where the pellet is inserted before it is shot.

bull—One black circle on the target.

butt plate—Mechanism on the back end of the stock that helps the rifle fit into the shoulder.

cant or canting—Placing the rifle in position at an angle so that the sights come more into the shooter's line of sight. Unless canting is consistent on each shot, the shooter will have shots that are off call even though they looked perfect.

cheek piece—Mechanism on the top of the back of the stock that helps the rifle fit the shooter's face and head.

chicken finger—A trigger finger that jumps off or forward of the trigger just as the rifle shoots the shot.

clear barrel indicator (CBI)—Monofilament cord or cord from a line trimmer that is inserted through the barrel so that it can be seen coming out the muzzle and breech of the rifle. This safety device shows that the rifle barrel is clear and can't be loaded.

cocking lever—Small lever on the side of the rifle used to open and close the action when the shooter is loading a pellet.

cross-fire—Shot that came from a shooter on a different point.

crown—Inside ring of the barrel at the muzzle end.

cutoff score—Minimum score needed to qualify for a particular match such as the Junior Olympics.

down range—Area of the range where the targets hang.

electronic target—Electronic system that calculates where a pellet hits on a grid based on the sound waves that it makes when going through a paper target.

eye relief—Distance from aiming eye to rear sight; should be 1 to 4 inches (2.5 to 10 centimeters).

final—The top eight shooters shoot 10 additional timed shots at the end of the regular course of fire to determine the winner.

firing line—Line immediately in front of the shooter that indicates where the proper distance to the targets begins (32 feet 9 3/4 inches, or 10 meters, from the firing line to targets for air rifle); the safety line that no one crosses unless the range officer has announced retrieval of targets.

firing point, or point—Area for each shooter to shoot from; each point has a number to indicate the shooter's place to shoot.

first stage—First part of the trigger pull that takes up the slack; stops at the second stage.

front sight—Sight on the front of the rifle that the shooter centers inside the rear sight and on the bull.

go for record—Term used when the shooter starts shooting at record bulls for score. After a shooter goes for record, he or she can't go back to the sighting bulls until the next target change.

jerking—Hard pull on the trigger that causes the whole rifle to move during the shot.

keeper—Loop around the top part of the sling to keep the opening around the arm secure and strong.

line is hot—Term that indicates that live firing is about to begin.

line is safe—Term that indicates that all rifles are grounded and unloaded and that going down range is safe when the line officer announces it.

line or range officer—Person in charge of the range and the shooters during a match.

match—Shooting competition that includes a set number of shots and positions for that particular shooting event.

match director—Person who organizes the match, puts together the match program and publishes it, takes the entry forms and fees, and designates the squadding for the relays.

miss (also called a zero or snowbird)—Shot that misses the black circle and is in the white of the target.

muzzle—Front of the barrel where the pellet comes out.

natural point of aim (NPA)—Where the shooter naturally points on the target when relaxed in position.

offhand stand—Small shooting stand on which to rest the rifle between shots while shooting standing and to hold pellets while in standing and kneeling positions.

overhold—Aiming and shooting past the time (about eight seconds) that the shot can be successful.

paper target—Paper with a certain number of bulls on it to shoot at.

pellet trap—Container or backstop to stop and catch pellets after they are shot through a target.

pistol grip—Rounded grip behind the trigger that the hand with the trigger finger holds during shooting.

precision air rifle—Highly accurate air rifle used in international and three-position air rifle shooting.

range commands—Specific commands called by the line officer to ensure that everyone is safe and following the rules of the match. Common commands include "Load and commence fire," "Start," "Cease fire," "Stop," and "Ground your rifles."

rear iris—Small opening in the rear sight that opens and closes to let more or less light into the eye for aiming.

rear sight—Sight mounted on the back of the rifle that the shooter looks through to begin the aiming process. The sight can be adjusted to move the strike of the pellet on the target.

relay—One group of shooters who shoot at the same time on the firing line for a match. Relay 1 refers to the first relay of shooters for the day. The relays progress until everyone has fired. Scores from all relays are then combined to determine overall match results.

rifling—Grooves and lands (raised areas) cut into the inside of the barrel in a twisting pattern to cause the pellet to spin on its way to the target to improve accuracy.

riser block—Small block that slides onto the sight rail in front and back and is tightened so that sights can be placed on top of it. The block raises the height of the sight to the shooter's eye.

rule books—Set of rules that a shooting program follows and that a match conforms to.

safety—Switch on the side of the rifle that locks the trigger.

second stage—Second part of the trigger pull; when the shooter pulls through this stage, the rifle fires.

shot plan—Specific plan that a shooter uses to shoot one successful shot.

sight alignment—Correctly centering the front sight in the rear sight.

sighters—Term for shots that are aimed at the sighting bulls.

sighting bull—Bulls (usually two) in the middle of the target that have a circle around them or a black triangle in the corner, indicating that they are to be used for sighting shots. A shooter uses these bulls to sight in the rifle before going for record.

small-bore rifle—A .22 caliber firearm.

sporter air rifle—Type of beginning model for competitive air rifle shooting.

squadding—Names on each relay for the match.

stock—Largest part of the rifle, it includes the fore end, cheek piece, pistol grip, and butt plate, and supports the barrel and action.

target holder—Frame of wood or metal used to take the target down range if the range has manually movable targets or used down range to attach and hold targets for shooting.

three-position air rifle—Air rifle matches that include shooting prone, standing, and kneeling.

timer—Clock or timepiece used to time a match.

training plan—Seasonal plans that include range training, match shooting, physical training, mental training, and breaks.

trigger—Mechanism with an armature that, when pulled, releases compressed air to propel a pellet down range.

trigger guard—Metal guard around the trigger area to protect the trigger from being accidentally bumped.

◧ Additional Resources

NATIONAL SHOOTING ORGANIZATIONS

National Rifle Association
11250 Waples Mill Road
Fairfax, VA 22030
www.nra.org

Contact the NRA Competitive Shooting Division at 703-267-1050, competitions@nrahq. org, or www.nrahq.org/compete. You can order an online rule book at materials.nrahq.org/go/ products.aspx?cat=Rulebooks. Find out about sanctioned matches at http://www.nrapublications.org/ssusa/images/SSUSA0808_CE.pdf. The link www.nrahq.org/compete/airgun.asp is a useful source of information about air gun shooting and competitions in each state. Check out www.nrahq.org/compete/calendar. asp?category=39 for a list of state sectionals for three-position air rifle. The people listed as contacts for these matches will be able to give you information on the shooting opportunities in your area as well.

For more information on the NRA National Team Air-Rifle Championships, visit www.nrahq. org/compete/nm_jr-airgun-champ.asp. For information about camps, go to www.nrahq.org/ education/training/junior_olympic_camps.asp. You can find college information by state for varsity teams, clubs, and ROTC at www.nrahq. org/compete/college_lookup.asp.

National Three-Position Air Rifle
Council
Camp Perry, P.O. Box 576
Port Clinton, OH 43452.
competitions@adcmp.com
Phone: 419-635-2141, ext. 1102
Fax: 419-635-2573

You can find the rules at www.odcmp.com/3P.htm.

USA Shooting
1 Olympic Plaza
Colorado Springs, CO 80909
719-866-4670
www.usashooting.org

The link www.usashooting.org/clubMap.php has an interactive map. Click on your state to find a list of clubs and teams, including some organizations previously mentioned. To find information on the National Junior Olympic Three-Position Air Rifle Championships, go to www.usashooting.org/viewRelease.php?id=92.

SPONSORS OF THREE-POSITION AIR RIFLE PROGRAMS

American Legion: 317-630-1249 or 317-630-1210; go to www.legion.org and click "legion programs."

Civilian Marksmanship Program (CMP): www.odcmp.com (main Web site); www.odcmp.com/Programs/SJD.htm (state contacts); www.odcmp.com/Programs/camp.htm (summer camps)

National 4-H Shooting Sports: www.4-hshootingsports.org (main Web site); www.4-hshootingsports.org/state_contacts.php (state contacts)

JROTC for Army, Navy, Marine Corps, and Air Force: check your local high school to see what JROTC programs they offer or check the CMP Web site.

COLLEGIATE GOVERNING ORGANIZATIONS

NCAA: web1.ncaa.org/eligibilitycenter/common

INTERNATIONAL SHOOTING ORGANIZATIONS

International Shooting Sports Federation (ISSF): www.issf-shooting.org

The ISSF is the international governing body for shooting sports including World Cups, world championships, and Olympic Games.

◱ About the Author

Courtesy of Launi Meili

Launi Meili has a long and distinguished career in rifle. Meili won gold at the 1992 Olympic Games in Barcelona and set three Olympic records in her career. She placed in the air rifle competition that year and had also placed in both air rifle and small bore at the 1988 Olympics in Seoul. Meili has also won the three-position rifle championship seven times while setting three world shooting records and numerous national records throughout her career.

In 1992, Meili turned to coaching. She was the assistant coach for the U.S. national rifle team from 1997 to 2000. She helped create the International Coach Certification Program, which is the highest coaching credential recognized by USA Shooting and the NRA. Meili then moved on to coach at the college level at the University of Nebraska. During that time she was inducted into the Shooting Hall of Fame. In 2007 Meili took on the challenge of being the head coach of the United States Air Force Academy NCAA rifle team.

STEPS TO SUCCESS SPORTS SERIES

ADVANCED SWIMMING Steps to Success

The *Steps to Success Sports Series* is the most extensively researched and carefully developed set of books ever published for teaching and learning sports skills.

Each of the books offers a complete progression of skills, concepts, and strategies that are carefully sequenced to optimize learning for students, teaching for sport-specific instructors, and instructional program design techniques for future teachers.

The *Steps to Success Sports Series* includes:

Archery STEPS TO SUCCESS
Kathleen Haywood · Catherine Lewis

Australian Football STEPS TO SUCCESS
Andrew McLeod · Trevor Jaques

Badminton STEPS TO SUCCESS
Tony Grice

Basketball STEPS TO SUCCESS
Hal Wissel

Bowling STEPS TO SUCCESS
Doug Wiedman

FENCING Steps to Success
ELAINE CHERIS

Field Hockey STEPS TO SUCCESS
Elizabeth R. Anders with Sue Myers

Golf STEPS TO SUCCESS
Paul G. Schempp · Peter Mattsson

ICE SKATING Steps to Success
KARIN KUNZLE-WATSON, STEPHEN J. DEARMOND

NETBALL Steps to Success
WILMA SHAKESPEAR

Racquetball STEPS TO SUCCESS
Dennis Fisher

Rifle STEPS TO SUCCESS
Launi Meili

RUGBY Steps to Success
TONY BISCOMBE PETER DREWETT

Self-Defense STEPS TO SURVIVAL
Katy Mattingly

Soccer STEPS TO SUCCESS
Joseph A. Luxbacher

SOCIAL DANCE Steps to Success
JUDY PATTERSON WRIGHT

Softball STEPS TO SUCCESS
Diane L. Potter / Lynn V. Johnson

SQUASH Steps to Success
PHILIP YARROW

Swimming STEPS TO SUCCESS
David Thomas

TABLE TENNIS Steps to Success
LARRY HODGES

TEAM HANDBALL Steps to Success
REITA E. CLANTON MARY PHYL DWIGHT

Tennis STEPS TO SUCCESS
Jim Brown

Volleyball STEPS TO SUCCESS
Bonnie Kenny / Cindy Gregory

Weight Training STEPS TO SUCCESS
Thomas R. Baechle · Roger W. Earle

To place your order, U.S. customers call
TOLL FREE **1-800-747-4457**
In Canada call 1-800-465-7301
In Australia call 08 8372 0999
In Europe call +44 (0) 113 255 5665
In New Zealand call 0064 9 448 1207
or visit **www.HumanKinetics.com/StepstoSuccess**

HUMAN KINETICS
The Premier Publisher for Sports & Fitness
P.O. Box 5076, Champaign, IL 61825-5076